ABOUT THE AUTHOR

Miguel de Cervantes Saavedra was born on 29th September 1547 in Spain. Although his father was a doctor, Cervantes's family lived in poverty. During his childhood, they often moved around Spain and, as a result of this, little is known about his early life.

After studying for a while in Madrid, Cervantes became a soldier at the age of twenty-one. In 1571, he took part in the battle of Lepanto, and lost the use of his left arm. While returning from military service, he was kidnapped by Barbary pirates and enslaved in Algiers for five years. After several attempts at escape, he was eventually ransomed and returned to Spain in 1580.

Five years later, Cervantes entered the civil service, working as a tax collector and government purchasing agent. However, irregularities with the accounts led to his imprisonment on two occasions.

By 1585, Cervantes had developed an interest in a literary career, and he published his first novel, *La Galatea*, that same year. He also wrote numerous plays in the years that followed. Despite this, literary success eluded him until the publication of *Don Quixote* in 1605. The success of this novel was such that an unauthorised sequel appeared, forcing Cervantes to write his own second part, published just one year before his death in 1615.

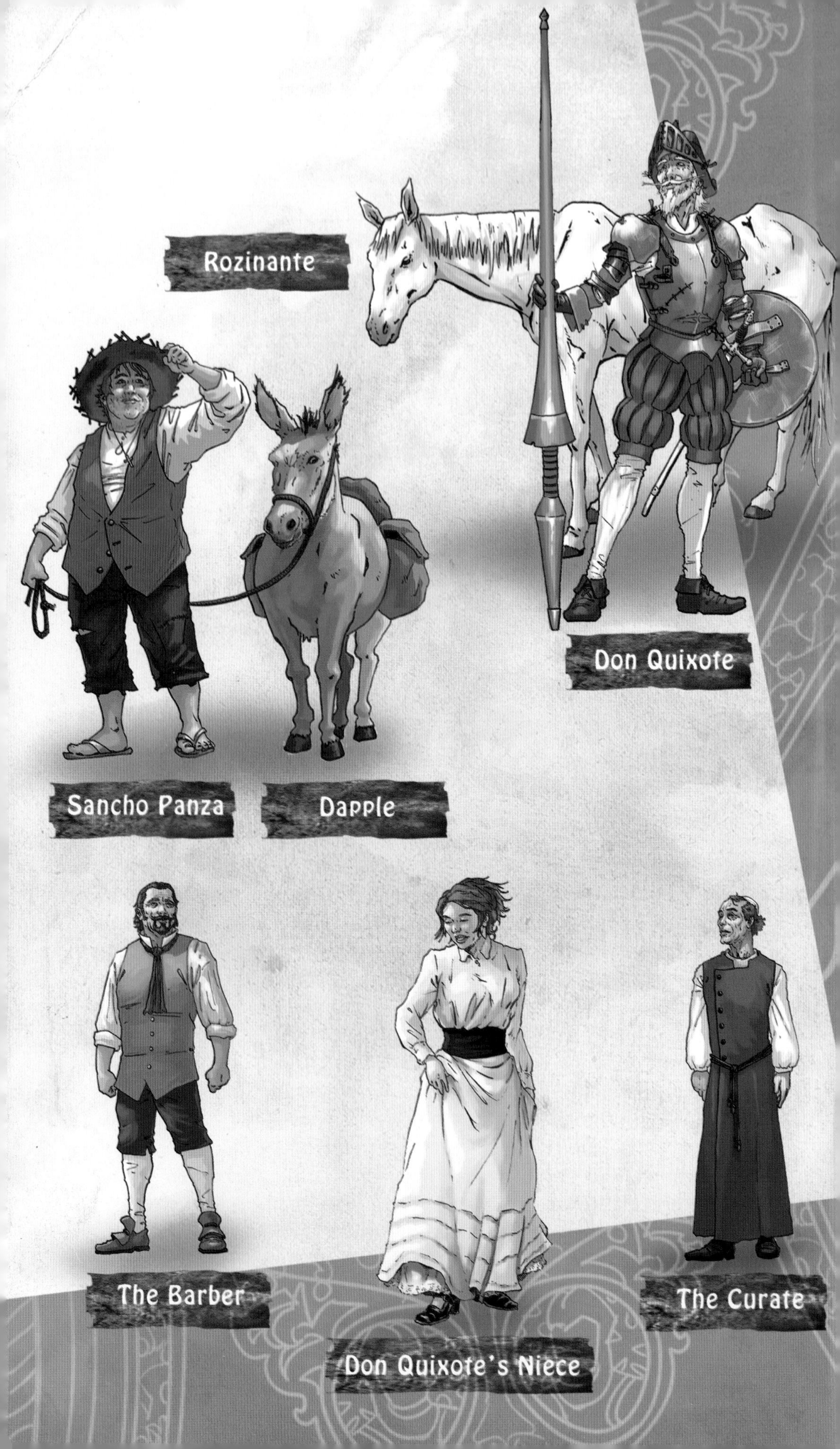
Rozinante
Don Quixote
Sancho Panza
Dapple
The Barber
The Curate
Don Quixote's Niece

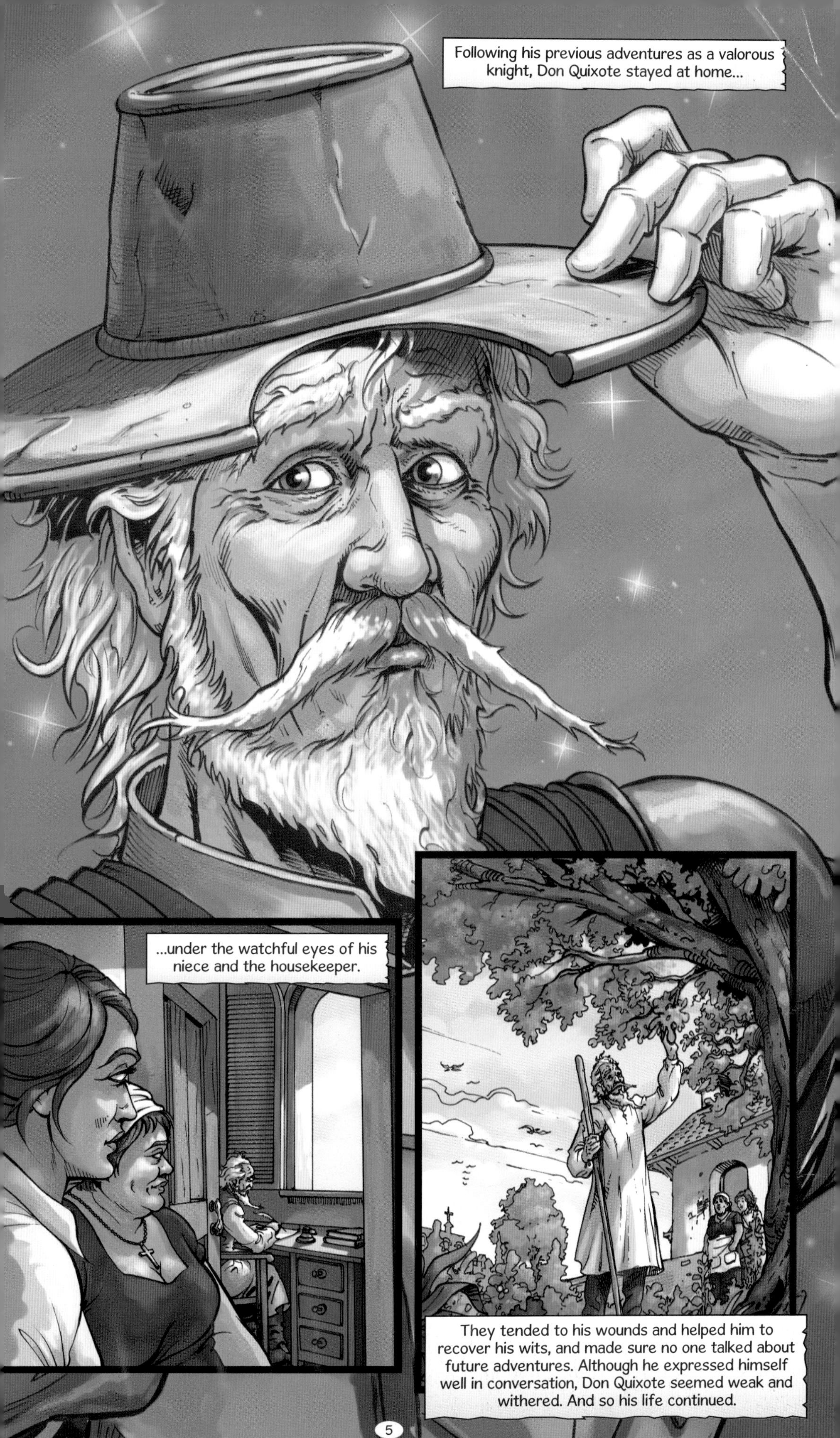
Following his previous adventures as a valorous knight, Don Quixote stayed at home...
...under the watchful eyes of his niece and the housekeeper.
They tended to his wounds and helped him to recover his wits, and made sure no one talked about future adventures. Although he expressed himself well in conversation, Don Quixote seemed weak and withered. And so his life continued.

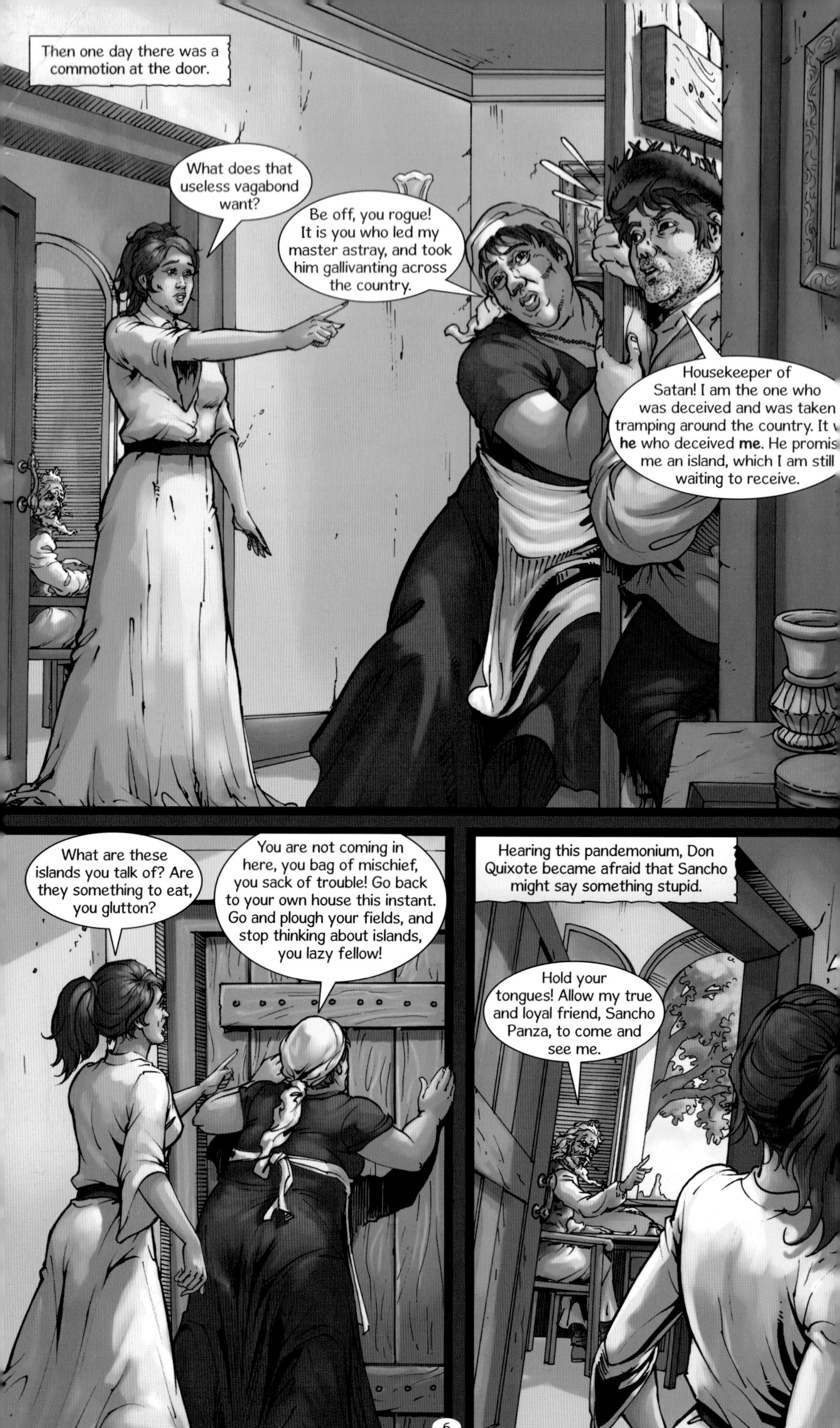
Then one day there was a commotion at the door.
What does that useless vagabond want?
Be off, you rogue! It is you who led my master astray, and took him gallivanting across the country.
Housekeeper of Satan! I am the one who was deceived and was taken tramping around the country. It
he who deceived **me**. He promis
me an island, which I am still waiting to receive.
What are these islands you talk of? Are they something to eat, you glutton?
You are not coming in here, you bag of mischief, you sack of trouble! Go back to your own house this instant. Go and plough your fields, and stop thinking about islands, you lazy fellow!
Hearing this pandemonium, Don Quixote became afraid that Sancho might say something stupid.
Hold your tongues! Allow my true and loyal friend, Sancho Panza, to come and see me.

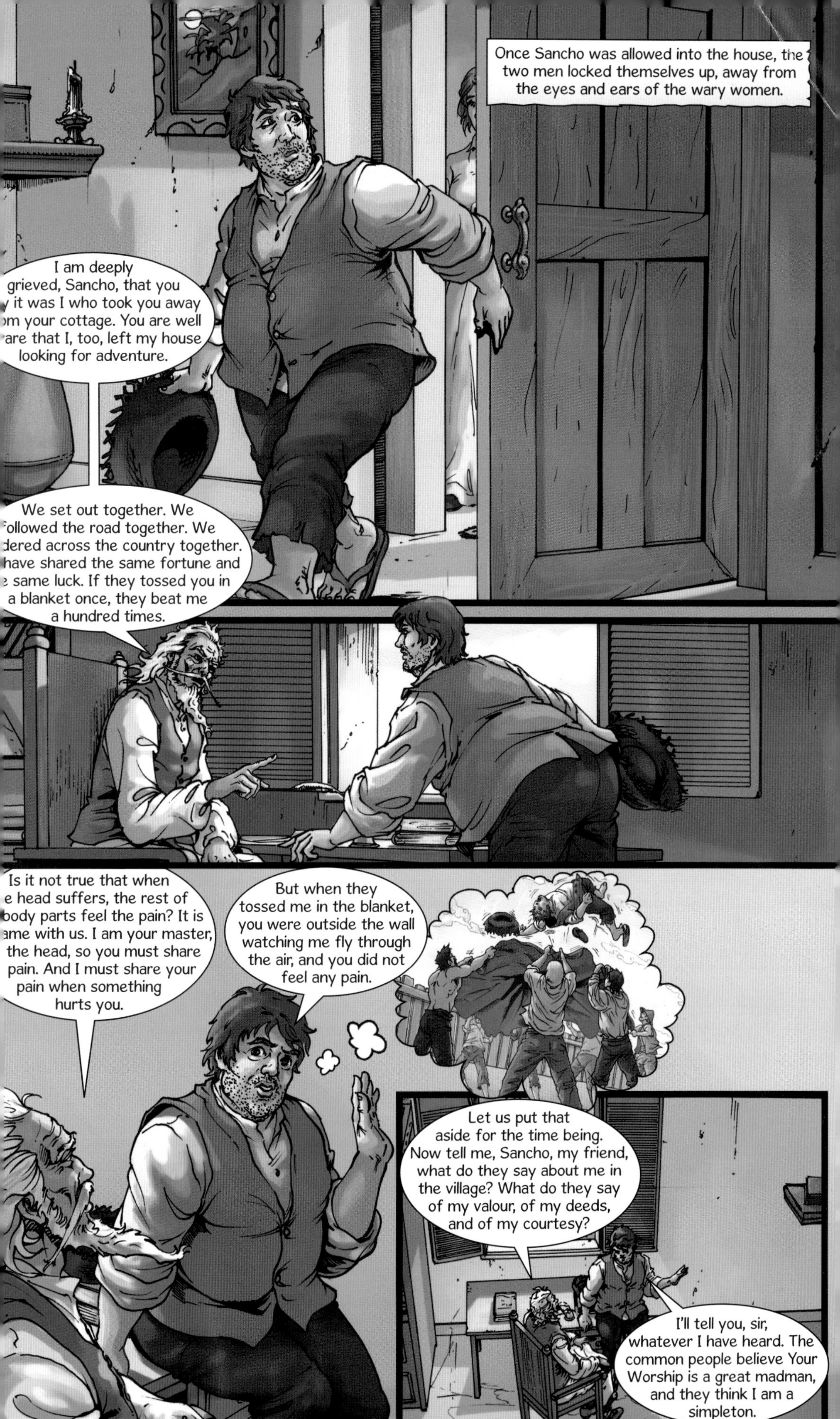
Once Sancho was allowed into the house, the two men locked themselves up, away from the eyes and ears of the wary women.
I am deeply grieved, Sancho, that you y it was I who took you away m your cottage. You are well are that I, too, left my house looking for adventure.
We set out together. We followed the road together. We dered across the country together. have shared the same fortune and same luck. If they tossed you in a blanket once, they beat me a hundred times.
Is it not true that when e head suffers, the rest of body parts feel the pain? It is ame with us. I am your master, the head, so you must share pain. And I must share your pain when something hurts you.
But when they tossed me in the blanket, you were outside the wall watching me fly through the air, and you did not feel any pain.
Let us put that aside for the time being. Now tell me, Sancho, my friend, what do they say about me in the village? What do they say of my valour, of my deeds, and of my courtesy?
I'll tell you, sir, whatever I have heard. The common people believe Your Worship is a great madman, and they think I am a simpleton.

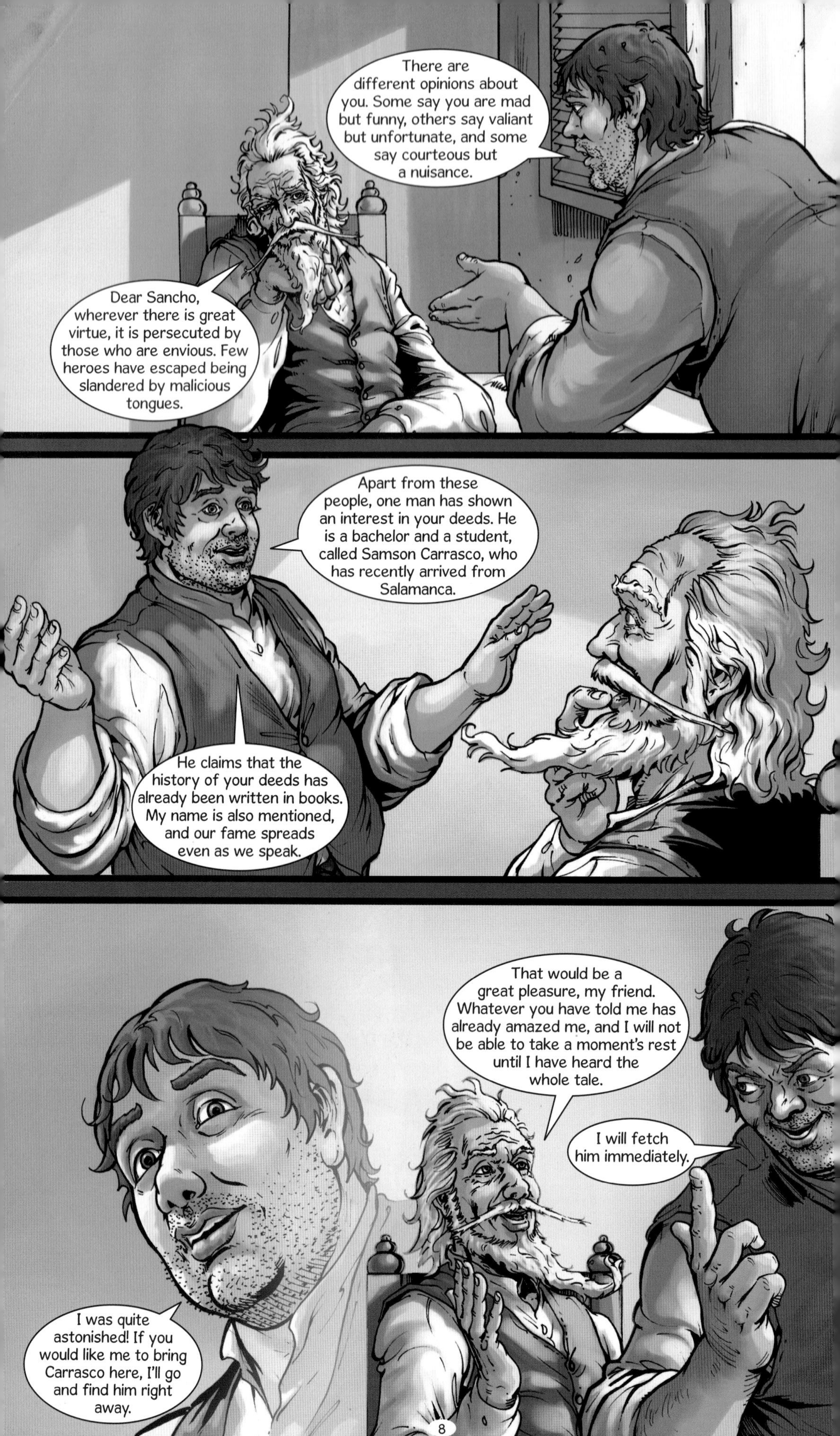

There are different opinions about you. Some say you are mad but funny, others say valiant but unfortunate, and some say courteous but a nuisance.
Dear Sancho, wherever there is great virtue, it is persecuted by those who are envious. Few heroes have escaped being slandered by malicious tongues.
Apart from these people, one man has shown an interest in your deeds. He is a bachelor and a student, called Samson Carrasco, who has recently arrived from Salamanca.
He claims that the history of your deeds has already been written in books. My name is also mentioned, and our fame spreads even as we speak.
I was quite astonished! If you would like me to bring Carrasco here, I'll go and find him right away.
That would be a great pleasure, my friend. Whatever you have told me has already amazed me, and I will not be able to take a moment's rest until I have heard the whole tale.
I will fetch him immediately.

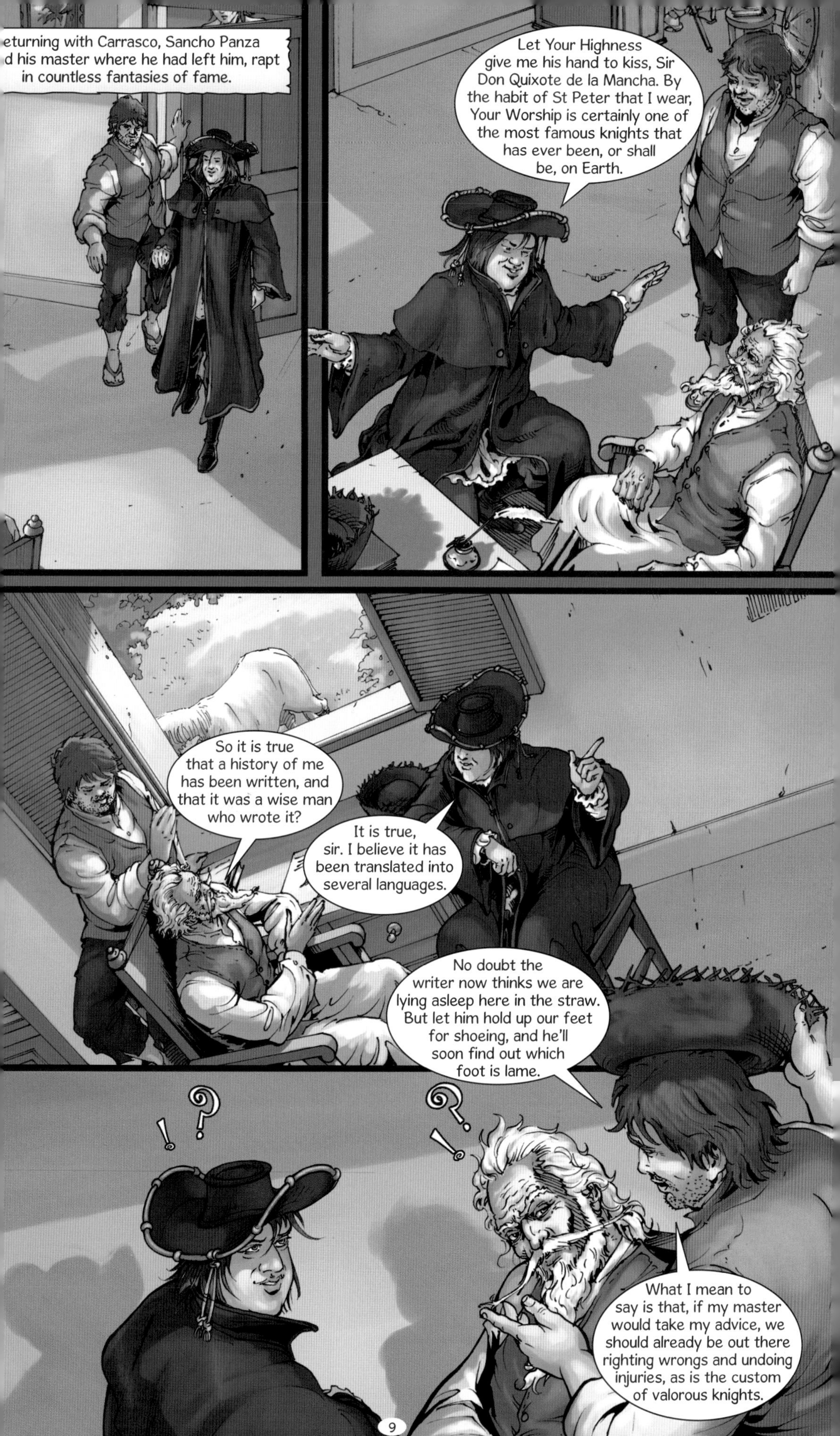
eturning with Carrasco, Sancho Panza d his master where he had left him, rapt in countless fantasies of fame.
Let Your Highness give me his hand to kiss, Sir Don Quixote de la Mancha. By the habit of St Peter that I wear, Your Worship is certainly one of the most famous knights that has ever been, or shall be, on Earth.
So it is true that a history of me has been written, and that it was a wise man who wrote it?
It is true, sir. I believe it has been translated into several languages.
No doubt the writer now thinks we are lying asleep here in the straw. But let him hold up our feet for shoeing, and he'll soon find out which foot is lame.
!?
?!
What I mean to say is that, if my master would take my advice, we should already be out there righting wrongs and undoing injuries, as is the custom of valorous knights.

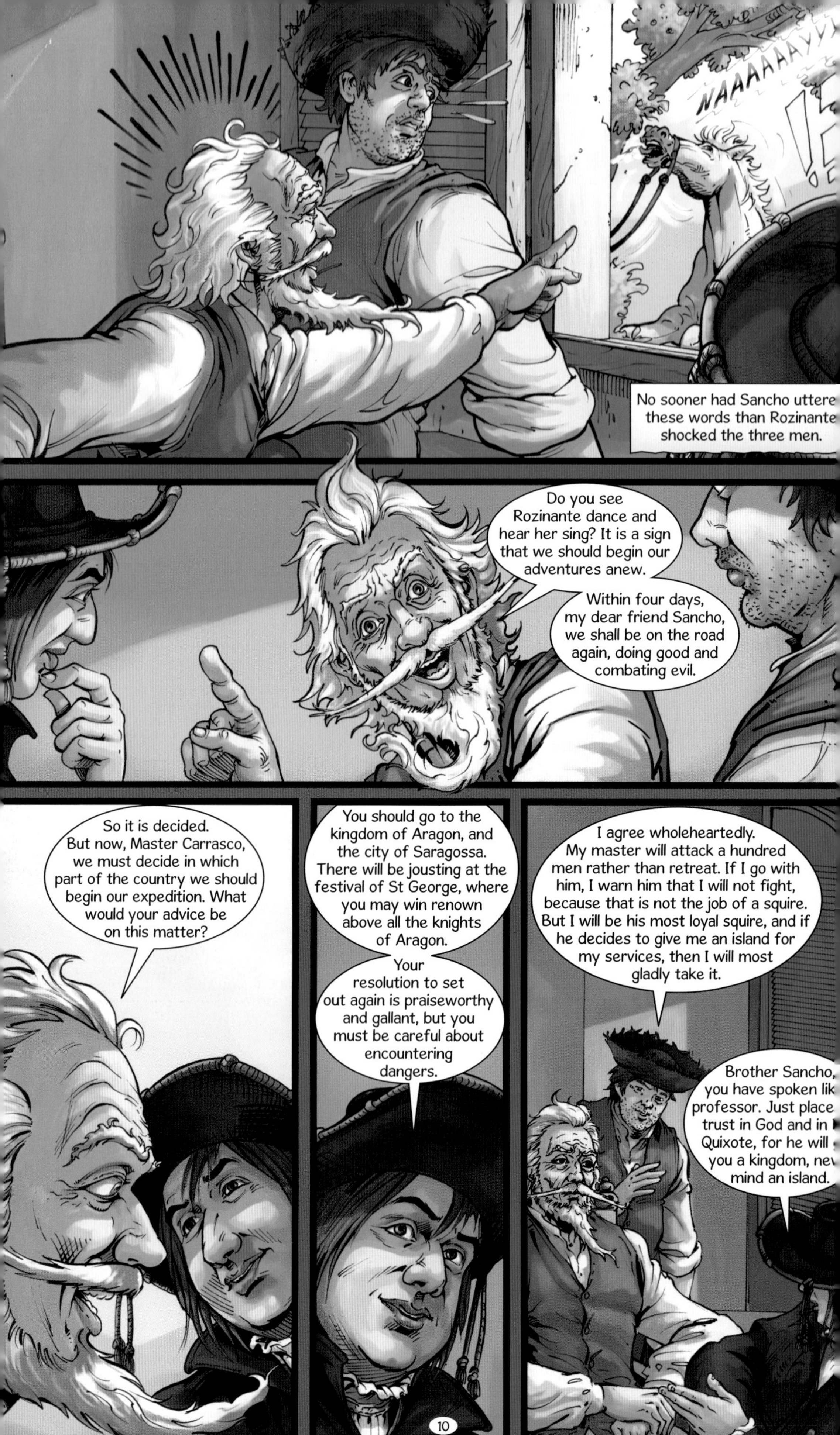
No sooner had Sancho uttere these words than Rozinante shocked the three men.
Do you see Rozinante dance and hear her sing? It is a sign that we should begin our adventures anew.
Within four days, my dear friend Sancho, we shall be on the road again, doing good and combating evil.
So it is decided. But now, Master Carrasco, we must decide in which part of the country we should begin our expedition. What would your advice be on this matter?
You should go to the kingdom of Aragon, and the city of Saragossa. There will be jousting at the festival of St George, where you may win renown above all the knights of Aragon.
Your resolution to set out again is praiseworthy and gallant, but you must be careful about encountering dangers.
I agree wholeheartedly. My master will attack a hundred men rather than retreat. If I go with him, I warn him that I will not fight, because that is not the job of a squire. But I will be his most loyal squire, and if he decides to give me an island for my services, then I will most gladly take it.
Brother Sancho, you have spoken lik professor. Just place trust in God and in Quixote, for he will you a kingdom, nev mind an island.

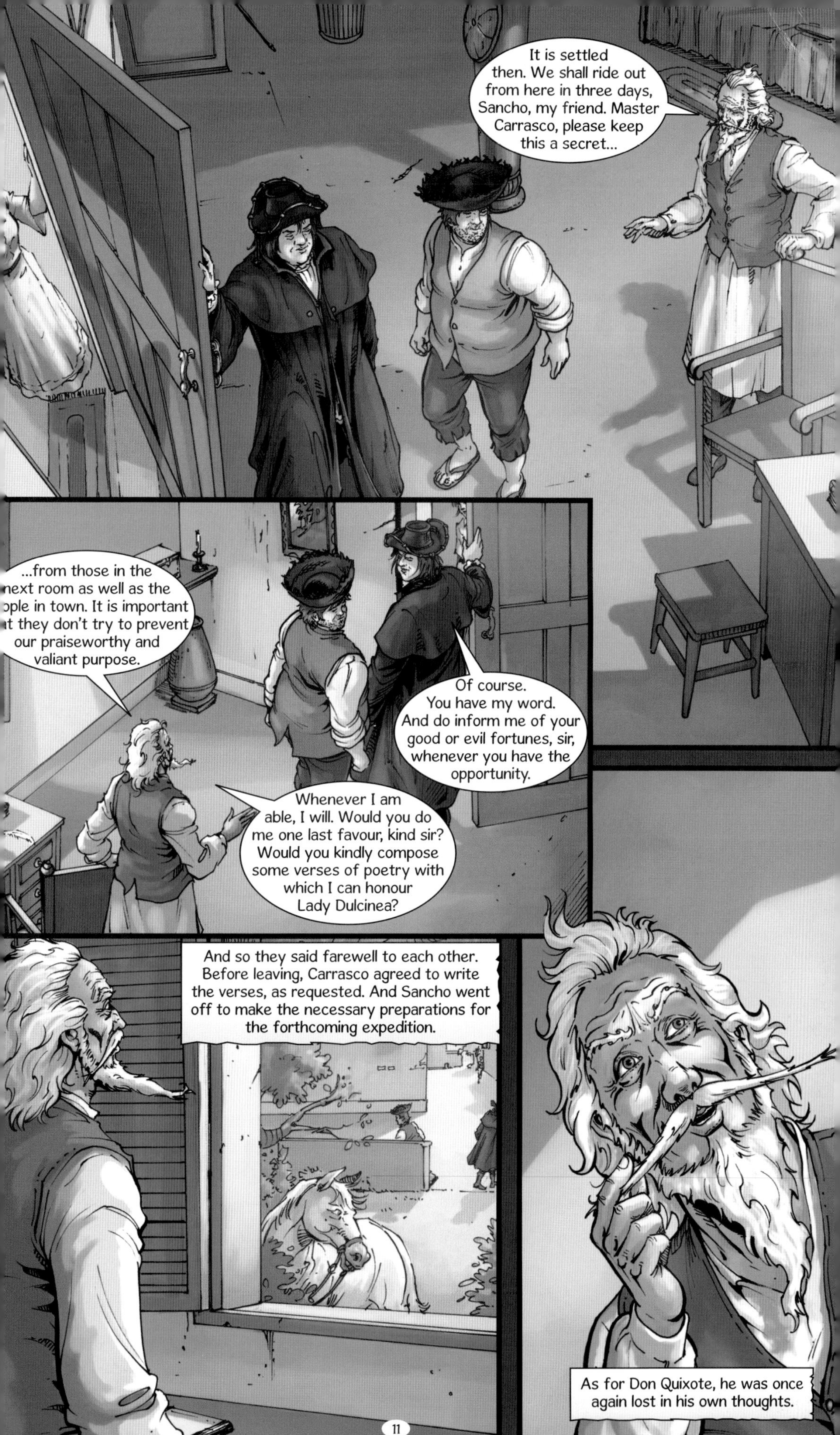

It is settled then. We shall ride out from here in three days, Sancho, my friend. Master Carrasco, please keep this a secret...
...from those in the next room as well as the ople in town. It is important t they don't try to prevent our praiseworthy and valiant purpose.
Of course. You have my word. And do inform me of your good or evil fortunes, sir, whenever you have the opportunity.
Whenever I am able, I will. Would you do me one last favour, kind sir? Would you kindly compose some verses of poetry with which I can honour Lady Dulcinea?
And so they said farewell to each other. Before leaving, Carrasco agreed to write the verses, as requested. And Sancho went off to make the necessary preparations for the forthcoming expedition.
As for Don Quixote, he was once again lost in his own thoughts.

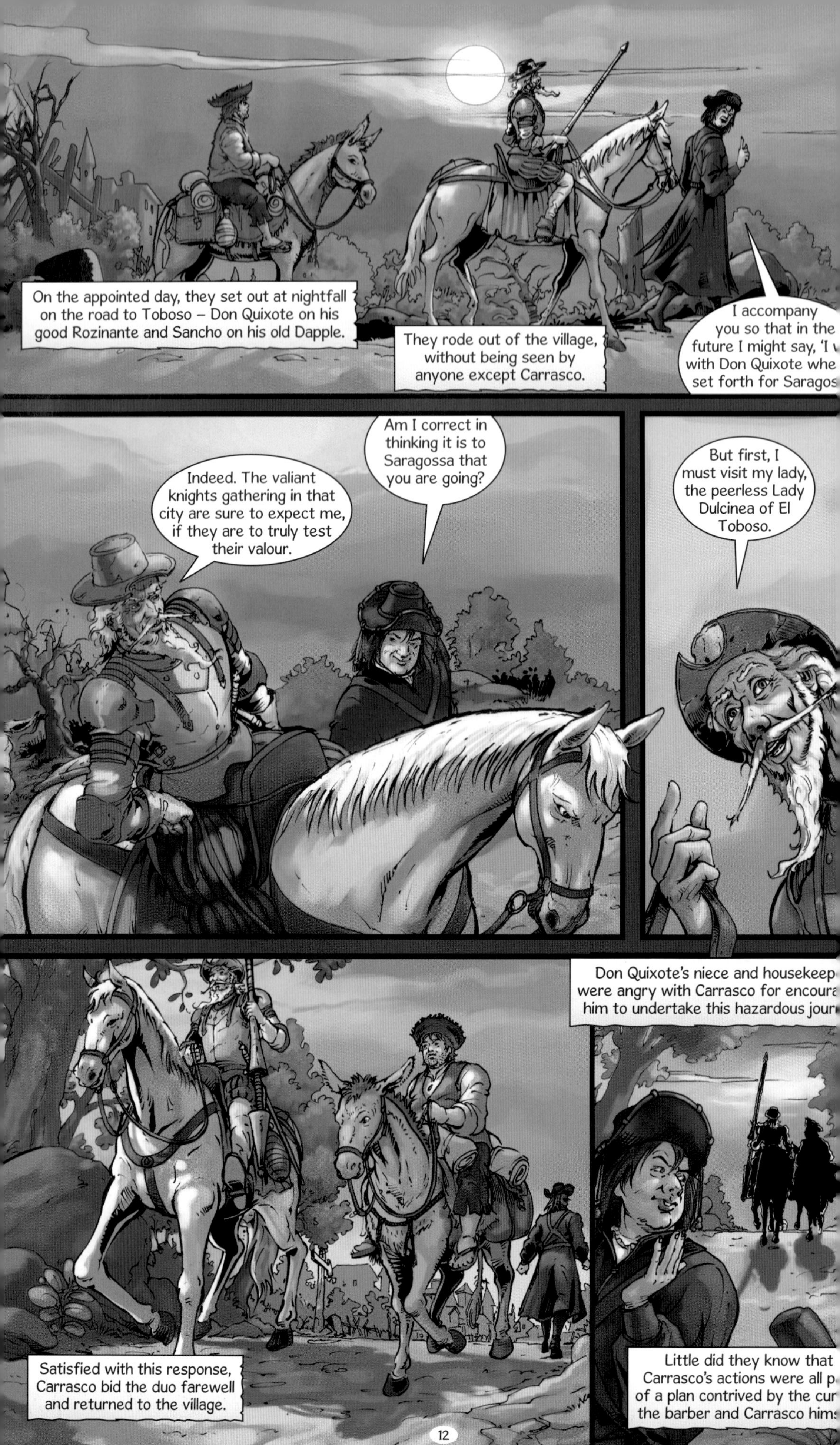
On the appointed day, they set out at nightfall on the road to Toboso – Don Quixote on his good Rozinante and Sancho on his old Dapple.
They rode out of the village, without being seen by anyone except Carrasco.
I accompany you so that in the future I might say, 'I
with Don Quixote whe
set forth for Saragos
Am I correct in thinking it is to Saragossa that you are going?
Indeed. The valiant knights gathering in that city are sure to expect me, if they are to truly test their valour.
But first, I must visit my lady, the peerless Lady Dulcinea of El Toboso.
Satisfied with this response, Carrasco bid the duo farewell and returned to the village.
Don Quixote's niece and housekeep
were angry with Carrasco for encour
him to undertake this hazardous jour
Little did they know that Carrasco's actions were all p
of a plan contrived by the cur
the barber and Carrasco him

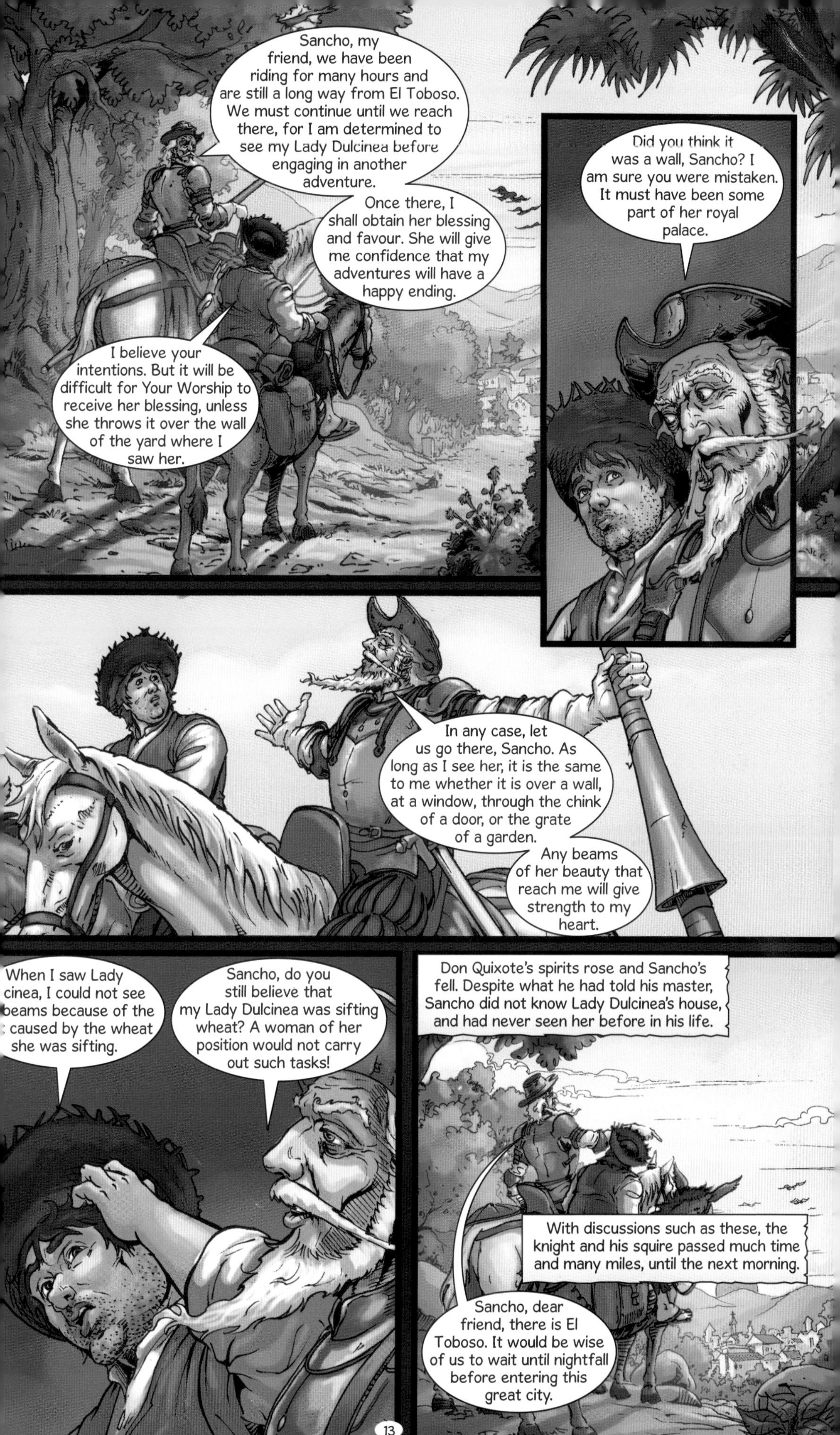
Sancho, my friend, we have been riding for many hours and are still a long way from El Toboso. We must continue until we reach there, for I am determined to see my Lady Dulcinea before engaging in another adventure.
Once there, I shall obtain her blessing and favour. She will give me confidence that my adventures will have a happy ending.
I believe your intentions. But it will be difficult for Your Worship to receive her blessing, unless she throws it over the wall of the yard where I saw her.
Did you think it was a wall, Sancho? I am sure you were mistaken. It must have been some part of her royal palace.
In any case, let us go there, Sancho. As long as I see her, it is the same to me whether it is over a wall, at a window, through the chink of a door, or the grate of a garden.
Any beams of her beauty that reach me will give strength to my heart.
When I saw Lady cinea, I could not see beams because of the caused by the wheat she was sifting.
Sancho, do you still believe that my Lady Dulcinea was sifting wheat? A woman of her position would not carry out such tasks!
Don Quixote's spirits rose and Sancho's fell. Despite what he had told his master, Sancho did not know Lady Dulcinea's house, and had never seen her before in his life.
With discussions such as these, the knight and his squire passed much time and many miles, until the next morning.
Sancho, dear friend, there is El Toboso. It would be wise of us to wait until nightfall before entering this great city.

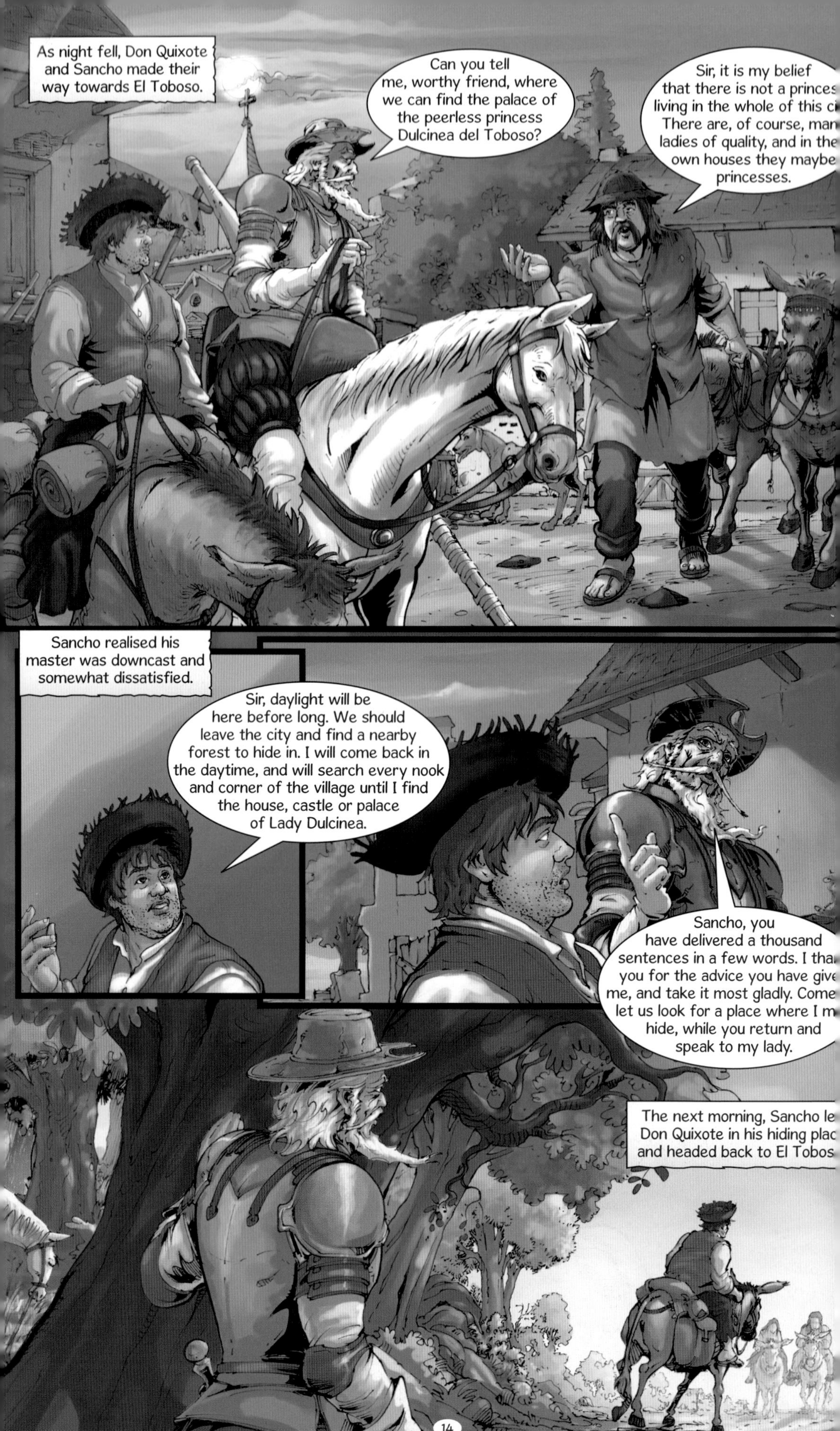
As night fell, Don Quixote and Sancho made their way towards El Toboso.
Can you tell me, worthy friend, where we can find the palace of the peerless princess Dulcinea del Toboso?
Sir, it is my belief that there is not a princes living in the whole of this ci There are, of course, man ladies of quality, and in the own houses they maybe princesses.
Sancho realised his master was downcast and somewhat dissatisfied.
Sir, daylight will be here before long. We should leave the city and find a nearby forest to hide in. I will come back in the daytime, and will search every nook and corner of the village until I find the house, castle or palace of Lady Dulcinea.
Sancho, you have delivered a thousand sentences in a few words. I tha you for the advice you have give me, and take it most gladly. Come let us look for a place where I m hide, while you return and speak to my lady.
The next morning, Sancho le Don Quixote in his hiding plac and headed back to El Tobos

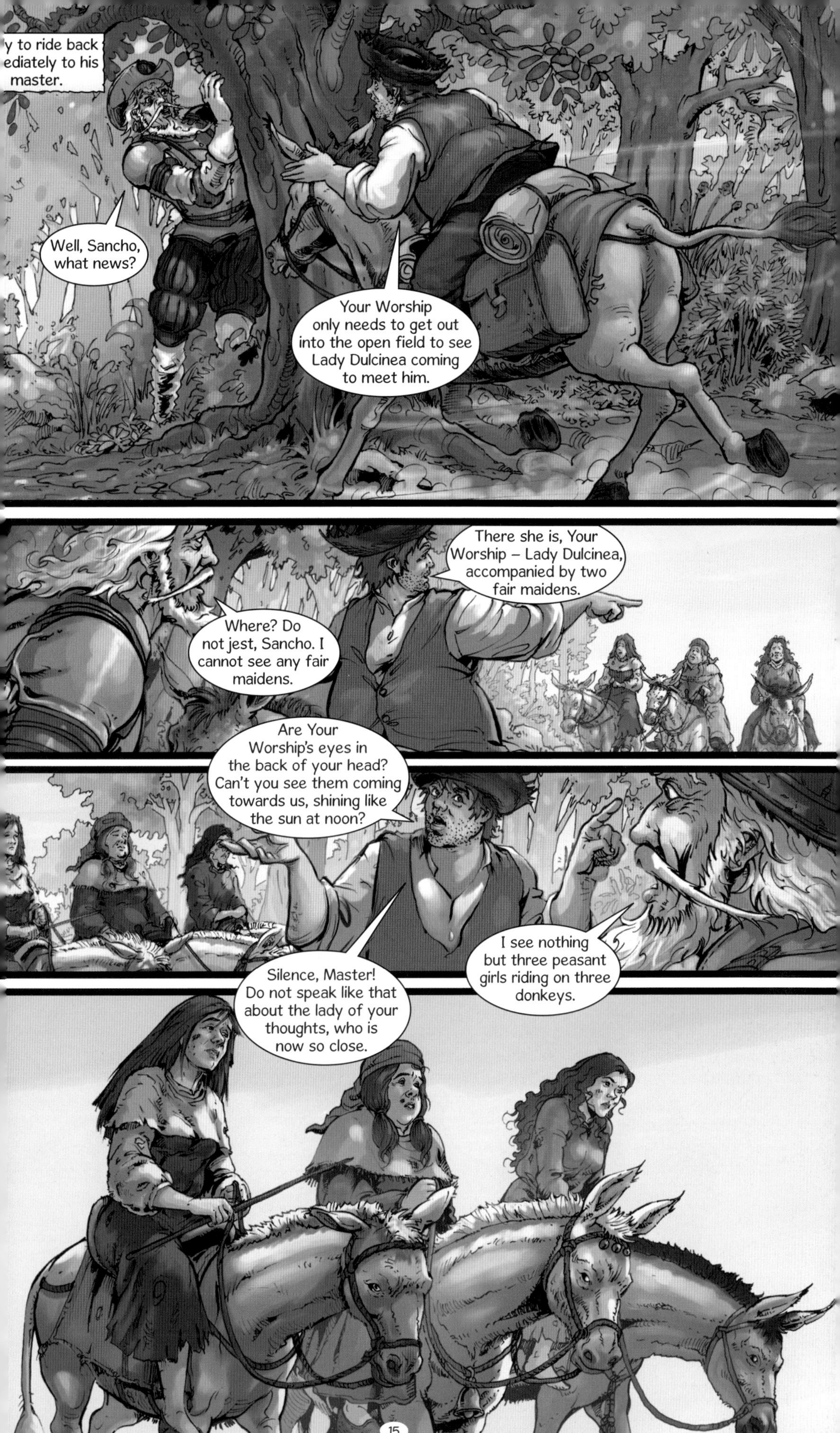
y to ride back
ediately to his
master.
Well, Sancho, what news?
Your Worship only needs to get out into the open field to see Lady Dulcinea coming to meet him.
There she is, Your Worship – Lady Dulcinea, accompanied by two fair maidens.
Where? Do not jest, Sancho. I cannot see any fair maidens.
Are Your Worship's eyes in the back of your head? Can't you see them coming towards us, shining like the sun at noon?
I see nothing but three peasant girls riding on three donkeys.
Silence, Master! Do not speak like that about the lady of your thoughts, who is now so close.

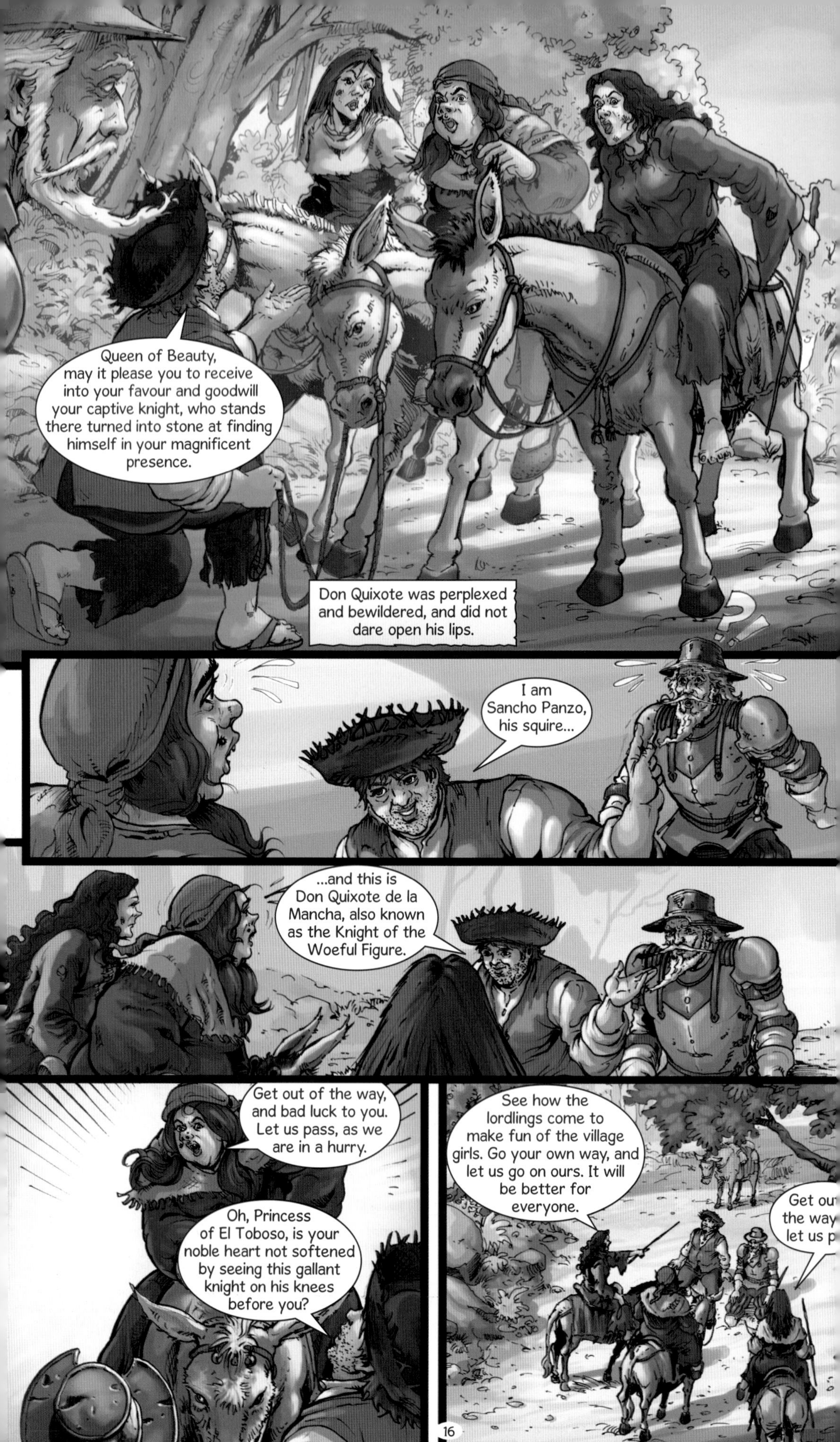
Queen of Beauty, may it please you to receive into your favour and goodwill your captive knight, who stands there turned into stone at finding himself in your magnificent presence.
Don Quixote was perplexed and bewildered, and did not dare open his lips.
?!
I am Sancho Panzo, his squire...
...and this is Don Quixote de la Mancha, also known as the Knight of the Woeful Figure.
Get out of the way, and bad luck to you. Let us pass, as we are in a hurry.
Oh, Princess of El Toboso, is your noble heart not softened by seeing this gallant knight on his knees before you?
See how the lordlings come to make fun of the village girls. Go your own way, and let us go on ours. It will be better for everyone.

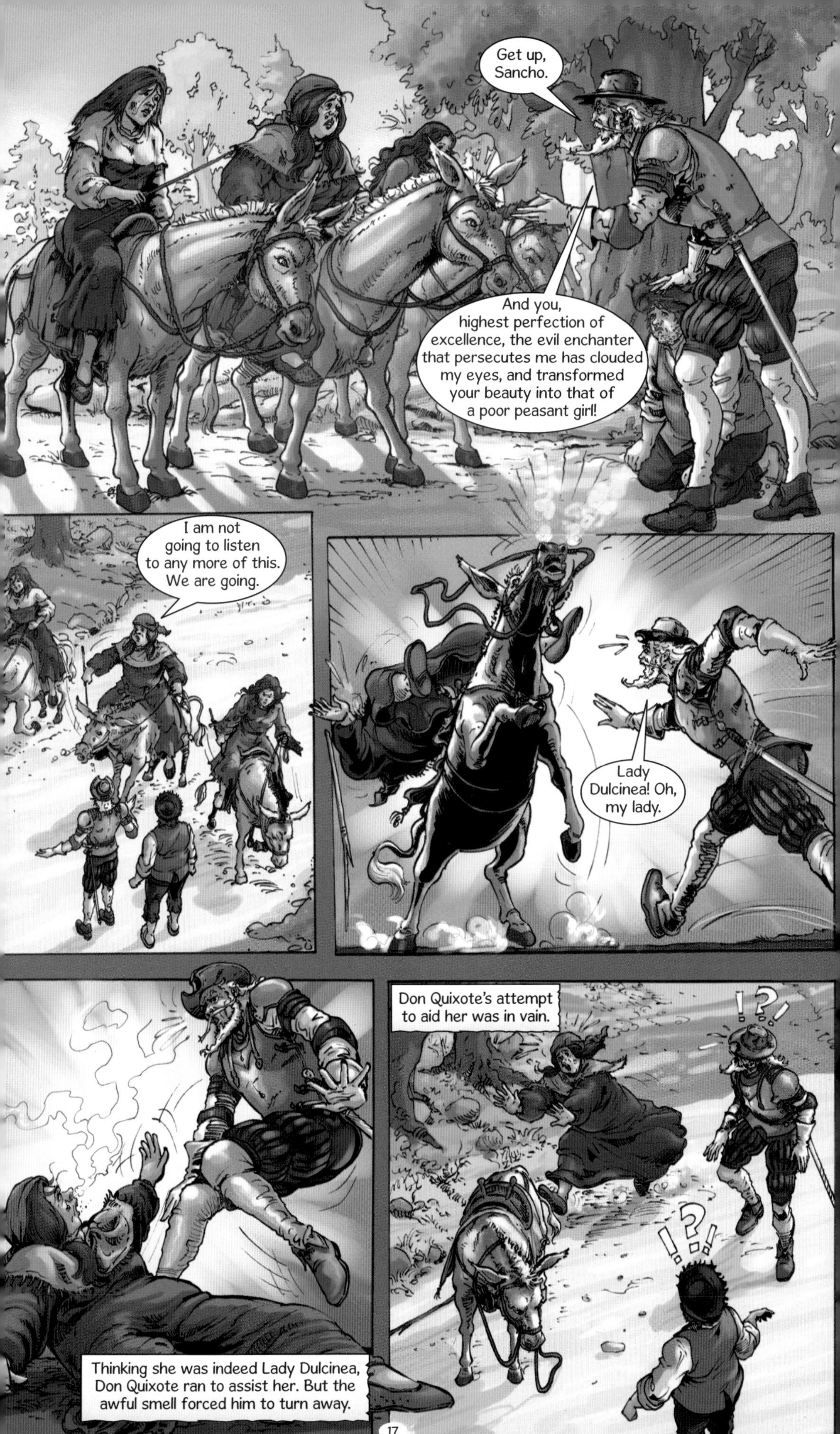
Get up, Sancho.
And you, highest perfection of excellence, the evil enchanter that persecutes me has clouded my eyes, and transformed your beauty into that of a poor peasant girl!
I am not going to listen to any more of this. We are going.
Lady Dulcinea! Oh, my lady.
Thinking she was indeed Lady Dulcinea, Don Quixote ran to assist her. But the awful smell forced him to turn away.
Don Quixote's attempt to aid her was in vain.
!?!
!?!

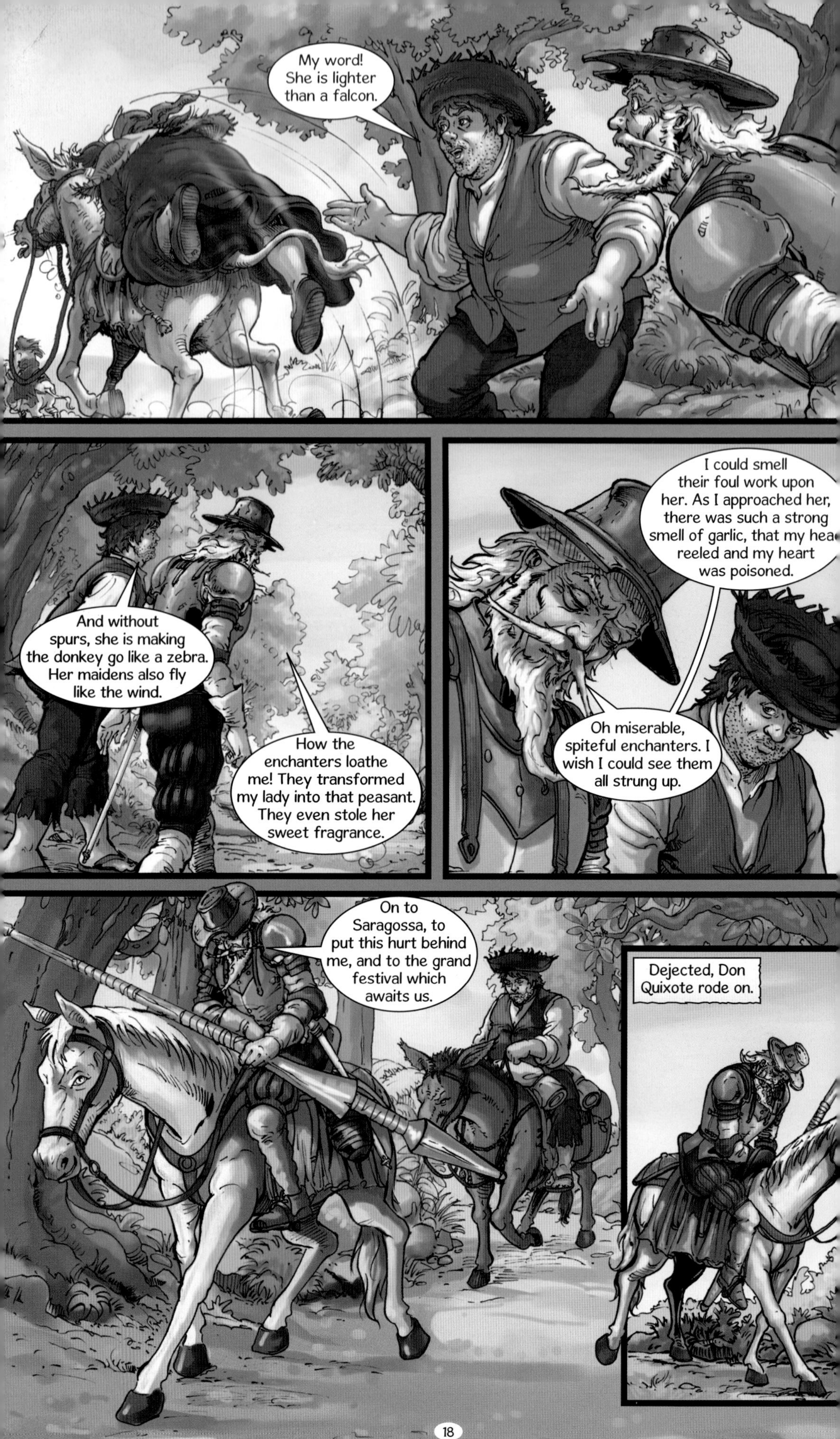
My word! She is lighter than a falcon.
And without spurs, she is making the donkey go like a zebra. Her maidens also fly like the wind.
How the enchanters loathe me! They transformed my lady into that peasant. They even stole her sweet fragrance.
I could smell their foul work upon her. As I approached her, there was such a strong smell of garlic, that my hea reeled and my heart was poisoned.
Oh miserable, spiteful enchanters. I wish I could see them all strung up.
On to Saragossa, to put this hurt behind me, and to the grand festival which awaits us.
Dejected, Don Quixote rode on.

e night, while Sancho slept,
n Quixote was disturbed by
noise coming from nearby.

Dismount, my friend, and take the bridles off the horses. This place has the silence and solitude that my lovesick thoughts need.

Don Quixote heard the sound of a man's armour and realised that he must be a brave knight.

Friend Sancho, we have an adventure.

Where?

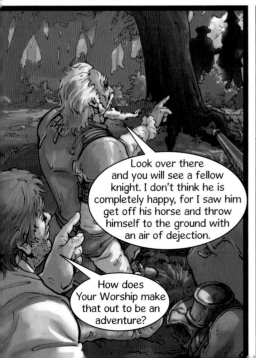

Look over there and you will see a fellow knight. I don't think he is completely happy, for I saw him get off his horse and throw himself to the ground with an air of dejection.

How does Your Worship make that out to be an adventure?

The knight heard their voices, and spoke in a distinct but courteous tone.

Who goes there? What are you? Do you belong to the number of the happy or of the miserable?

Of the miserable.

Then come to me.

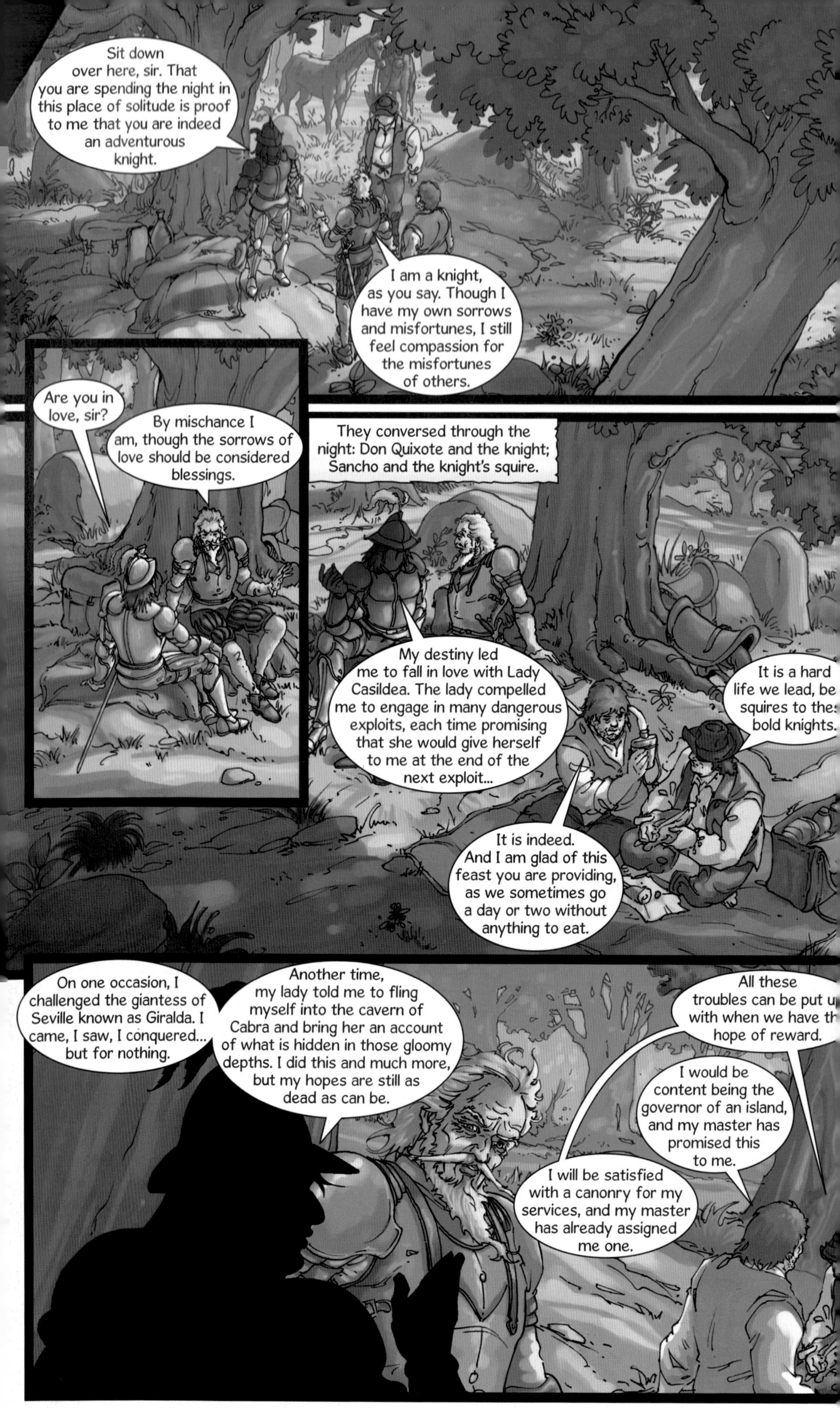
Sit down over here, sir. That you are spending the night in this place of solitude is proof to me that you are indeed an adventurous knight.
I am a knight, as you say. Though I have my own sorrows and misfortunes, I still feel compassion for the misfortunes of others.
Are you in love, sir?
By mischance I am, though the sorrows of love should be considered blessings.
They conversed through the night: Don Quixote and the knight; Sancho and the knight's squire.
My destiny led me to fall in love with Lady Casildea. The lady compelled me to engage in many dangerous exploits, each time promising that she would give herself to me at the end of the next exploit...
It is a hard life we lead, be squires to the bold knights.
It is indeed. And I am glad of this feast you are providing, as we sometimes go a day or two without anything to eat.
On one occasion, I challenged the giantess of Seville known as Giralda. I came, I saw, I conquered... but for nothing.
Another time, my lady told me to fling myself into the cavern of Cabra and bring her an account of what is hidden in those gloomy depths. I did this and much more, but my hopes are still as dead as can be.
All these troubles can be put u with when we have th hope of reward.
I would be content being the governor of an island, and my master has promised this to me.
I will be satisfied with a canonry for my services, and my master has already assigned me one.

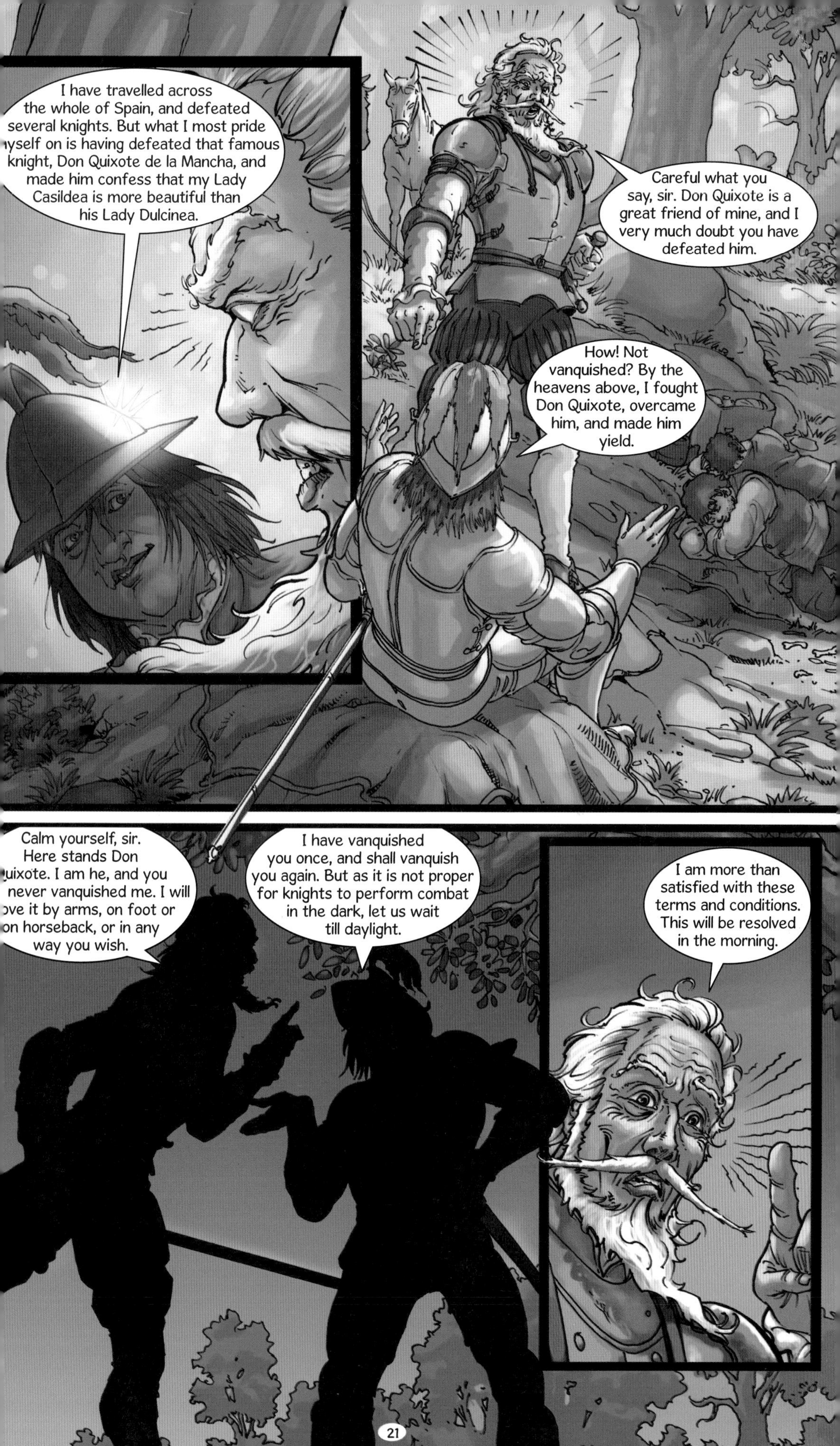

I have travelled across the whole of Spain, and defeated several knights. But what I most pride yself on is having defeated that famous knight, Don Quixote de la Mancha, and made him confess that my Lady Casildea is more beautiful than his Lady Dulcinea.
Careful what you say, sir. Don Quixote is a great friend of mine, and I very much doubt you have defeated him.
How! Not vanquished? By the heavens above, I fought Don Quixote, overcame him, and made him yield.
Calm yourself, sir. Here stands Don uixote. I am he, and you never vanquished me. I will ove it by arms, on foot or on horseback, or in any way you wish.
I have vanquished you once, and shall vanquish you again. But as it is not proper for knights to perform combat in the dark, let us wait till daylight.
I am more than satisfied with these terms and conditions. This will be resolved in the morning.

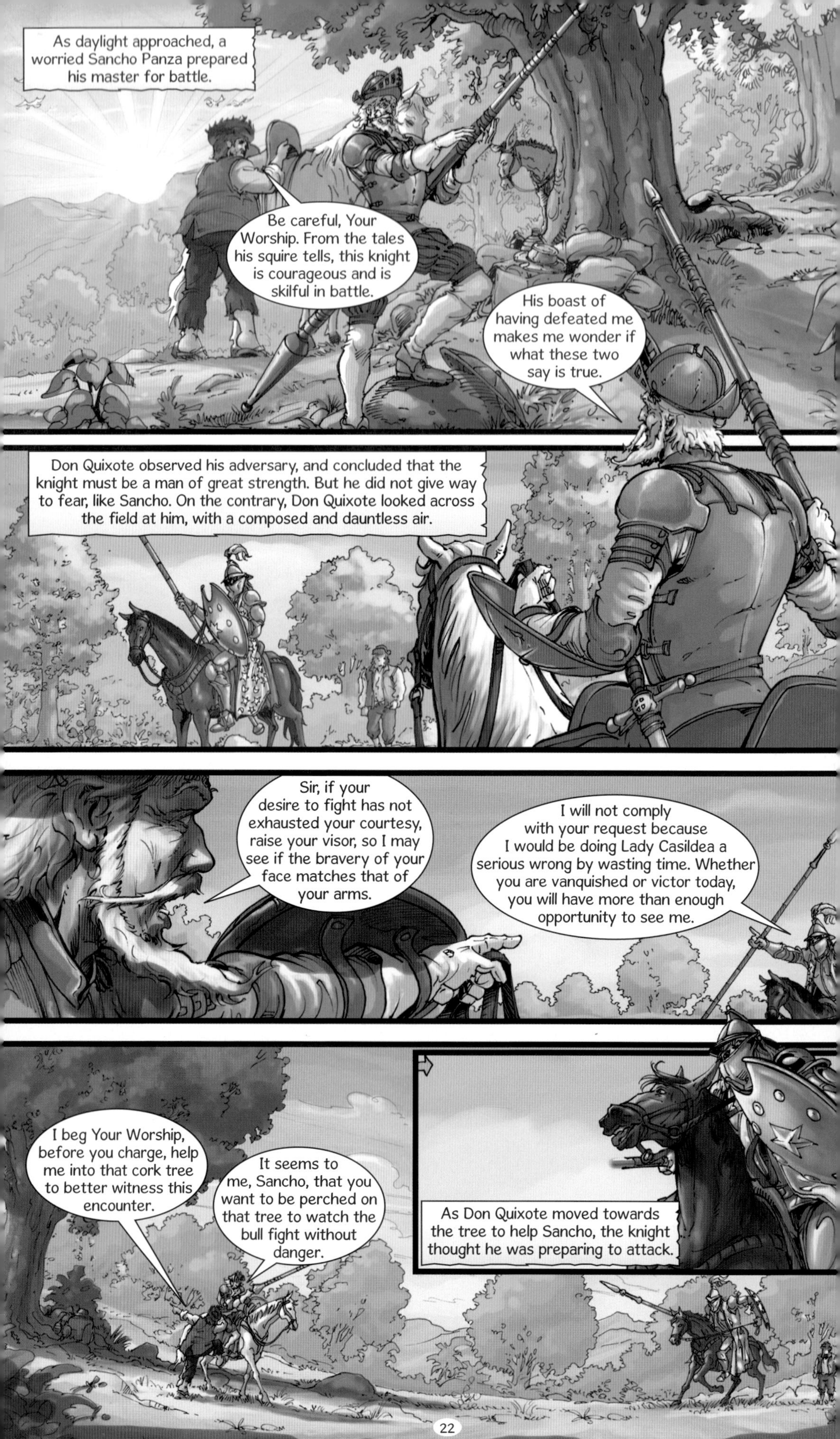

As daylight approached, a worried Sancho Panza prepared his master for battle.
Be careful, Your Worship. From the tales his squire tells, this knight is courageous and is skilful in battle.
His boast of having defeated me makes me wonder if what these two say is true.
Don Quixote observed his adversary, and concluded that the knight must be a man of great strength. But he did not give way to fear, like Sancho. On the contrary, Don Quixote looked across the field at him, with a composed and dauntless air.
Sir, if your desire to fight has not exhausted your courtesy, raise your visor, so I may see if the bravery of your face matches that of your arms.
I will not comply with your request because I would be doing Lady Casildea a serious wrong by wasting time. Whether you are vanquished or victor today, you will have more than enough opportunity to see me.
I beg Your Worship, before you charge, help me into that cork tree to better witness this encounter.
It seems to me, Sancho, that you want to be perched on that tree to watch the bull fight without danger.
As Don Quixote moved towards the tree to help Sancho, the knight thought he was preparing to attack.

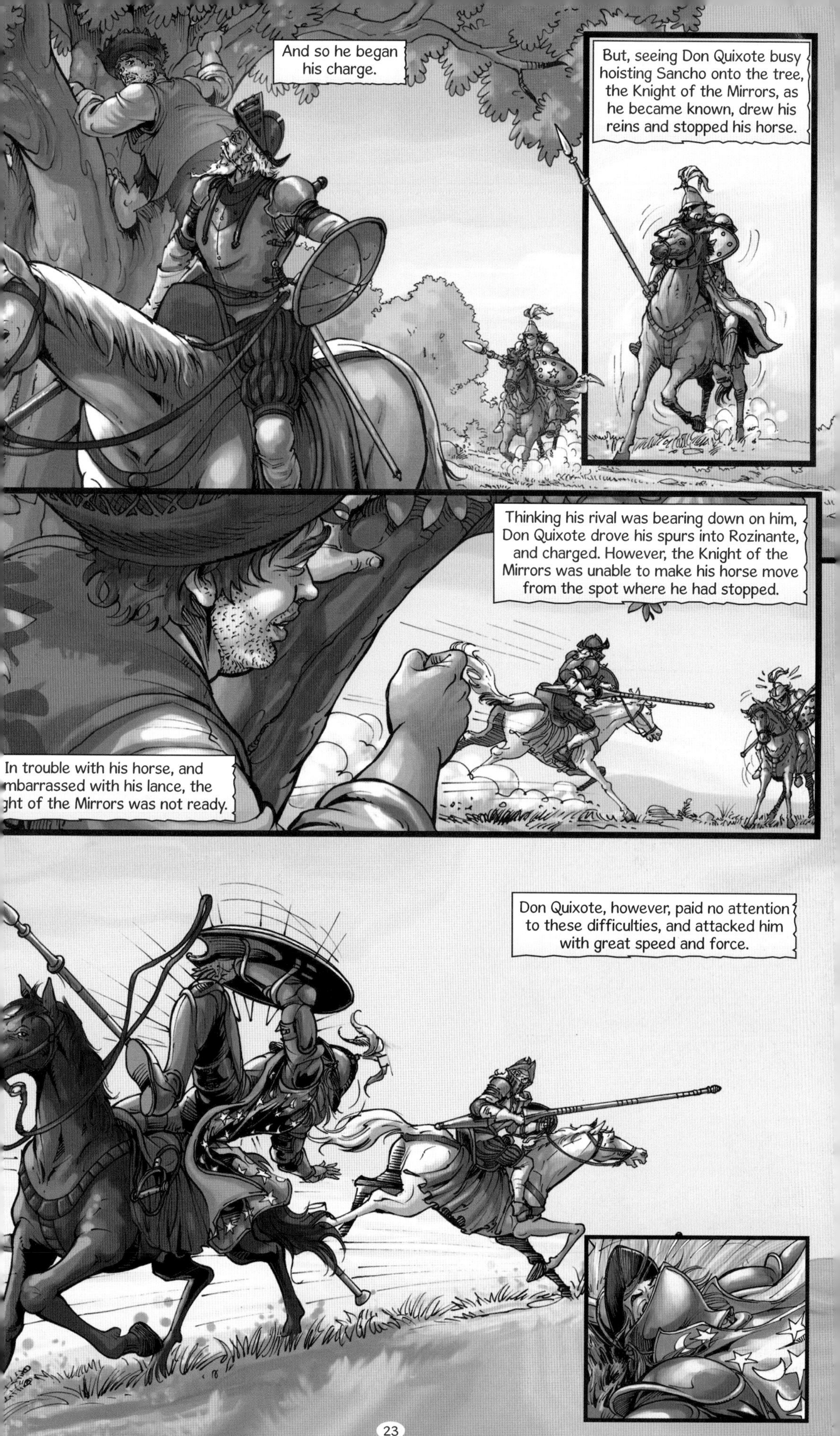
And so he began his charge.
But, seeing Don Quixote busy hoisting Sancho onto the tree, the Knight of the Mirrors, as he became known, drew his reins and stopped his horse.
Thinking his rival was bearing down on him, Don Quixote drove his spurs into Rozinante, and charged. However, the Knight of the Mirrors was unable to make his horse move from the spot where he had stopped.
In trouble with his horse, and mbarrassed with his lance, the ght of the Mirrors was not ready.
Don Quixote, however, paid no attention to these difficulties, and attacked him with great speed and force.

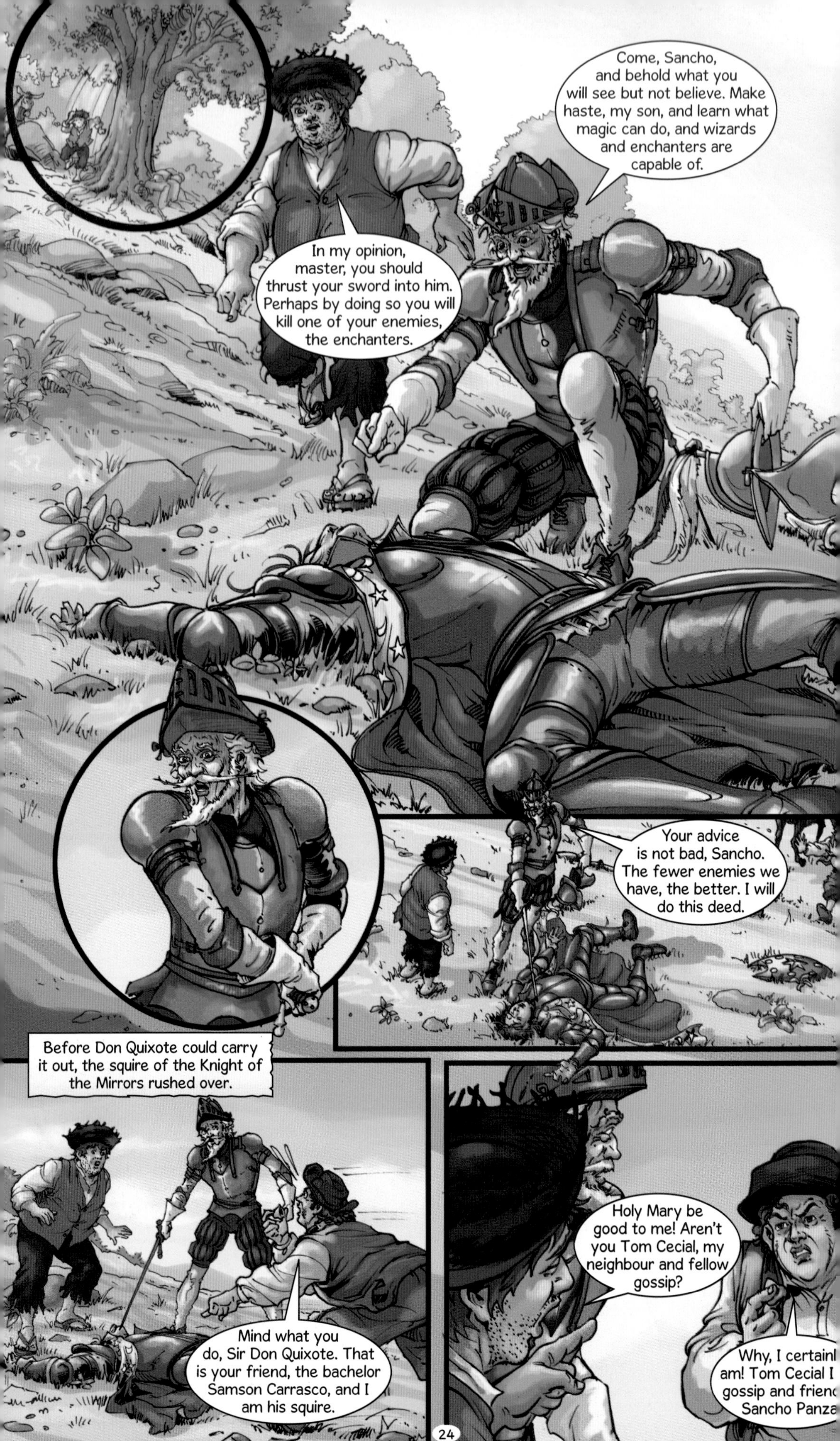
Come, Sancho, and behold what you will see but not believe. Make haste, my son, and learn what magic can do, and wizards and enchanters are capable of.
In my opinion, master, you should thrust your sword into him. Perhaps by doing so you will kill one of your enemies, the enchanters.
Your advice is not bad, Sancho. The fewer enemies we have, the better. I will do this deed.
Before Don Quixote could carry it out, the squire of the Knight of the Mirrors rushed over.
Mind what you do, Sir Don Quixote. That is your friend, the bachelor Samson Carrasco, and I am his squire.
Holy Mary be good to me! Aren't you Tom Cecial, my neighbour and fellow gossip?
Why, I certainl am! Tom Cecial I gossip and frienc Sancho Panza

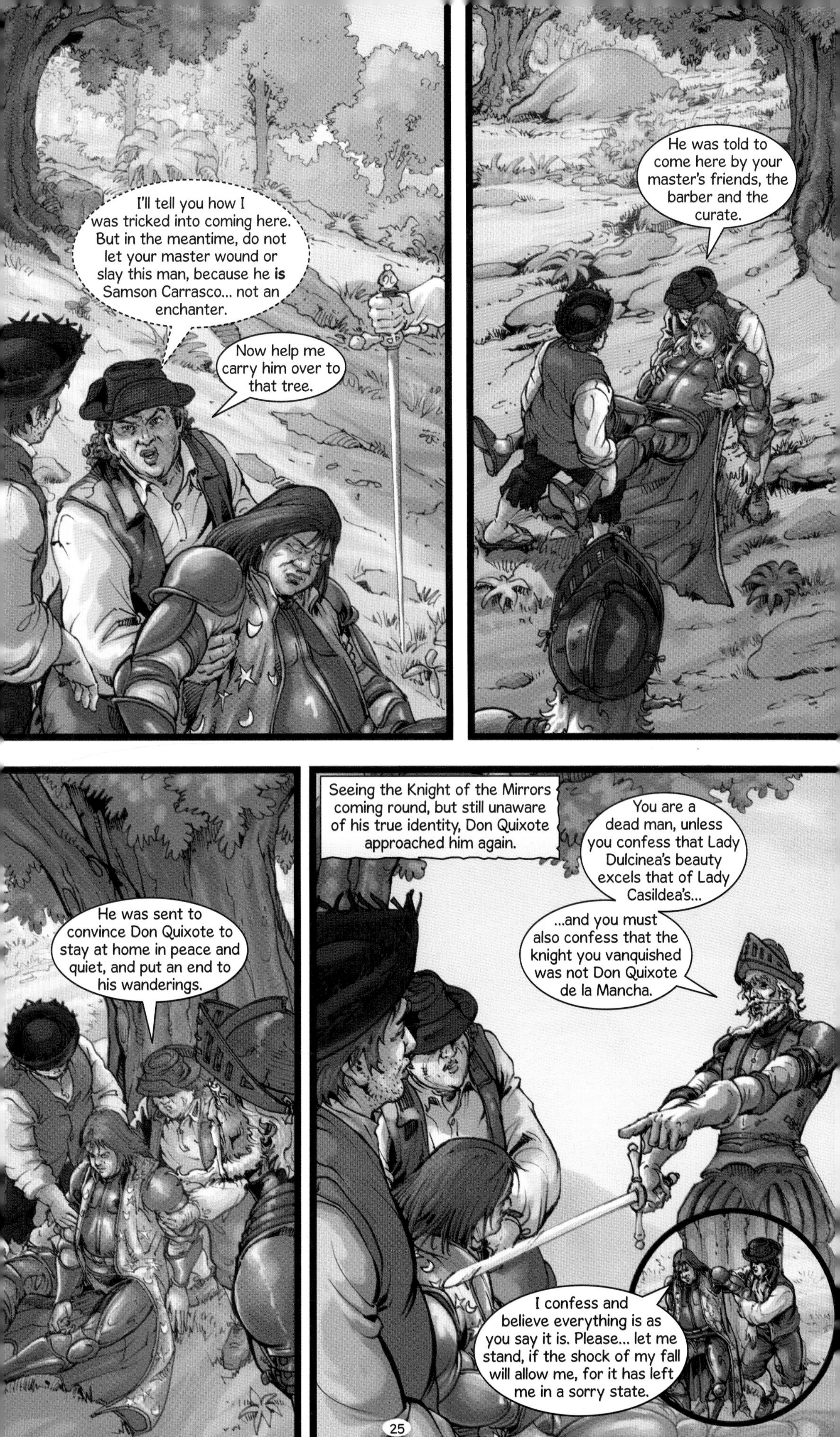
I'll tell you how I was tricked into coming here. But in the meantime, do not let your master wound or slay this man, because he **is** Samson Carrasco... not an enchanter.
Now help me carry him over to that tree.
He was told to come here by your master's friends, the barber and the curate.
He was sent to convince Don Quixote to stay at home in peace and quiet, and put an end to his wanderings.
Seeing the Knight of the Mirrors coming round, but still unaware of his true identity, Don Quixote approached him again.
You are a dead man, unless you confess that Lady Dulcinea's beauty excels that of Lady Casildea's...
...and you must also confess that the knight you vanquished was not Don Quixote de la Mancha.
I confess and believe everything is as you say it is. Please... let me stand, if the shock of my fall will allow me, for it has left me in a sorry state.

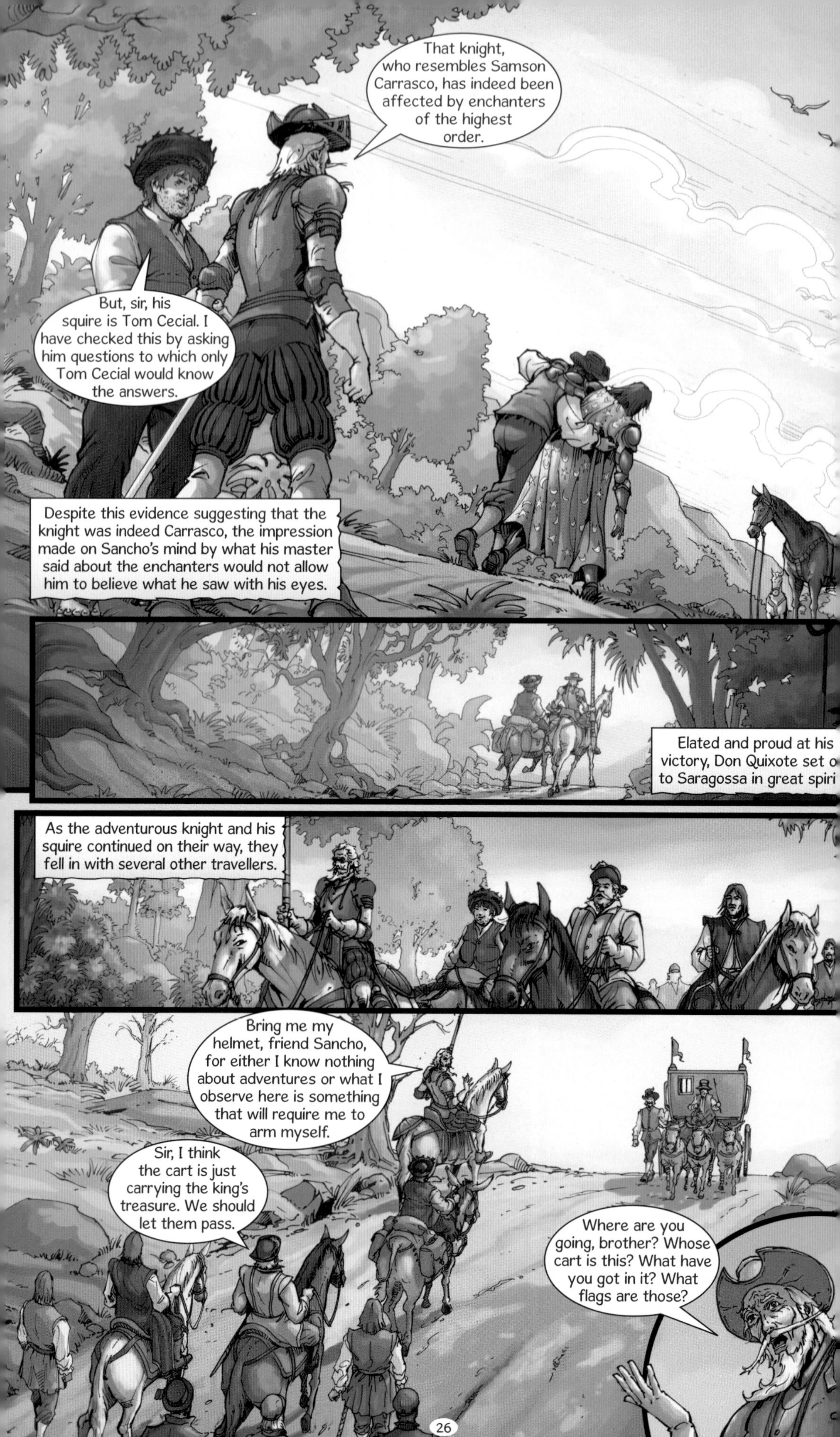
That knight, who resembles Samson Carrasco, has indeed been affected by enchanters of the highest order.
But, sir, his squire is Tom Cecial. I have checked this by asking him questions to which only Tom Cecial would know the answers.
Despite this evidence suggesting that the knight was indeed Carrasco, the impression made on Sancho's mind by what his master said about the enchanters would not allow him to believe what he saw with his eyes.
Elated and proud at his victory, Don Quixote set o to Saragossa in great spiri
As the adventurous knight and his squire continued on their way, they fell in with several other travellers.
Bring me my helmet, friend Sancho, for either I know nothing about adventures or what I observe here is something that will require me to arm myself.
Sir, I think the cart is just carrying the king's treasure. We should let them pass.
Where are you going, brother? Whose cart is this? What have you got in it? What flags are those?

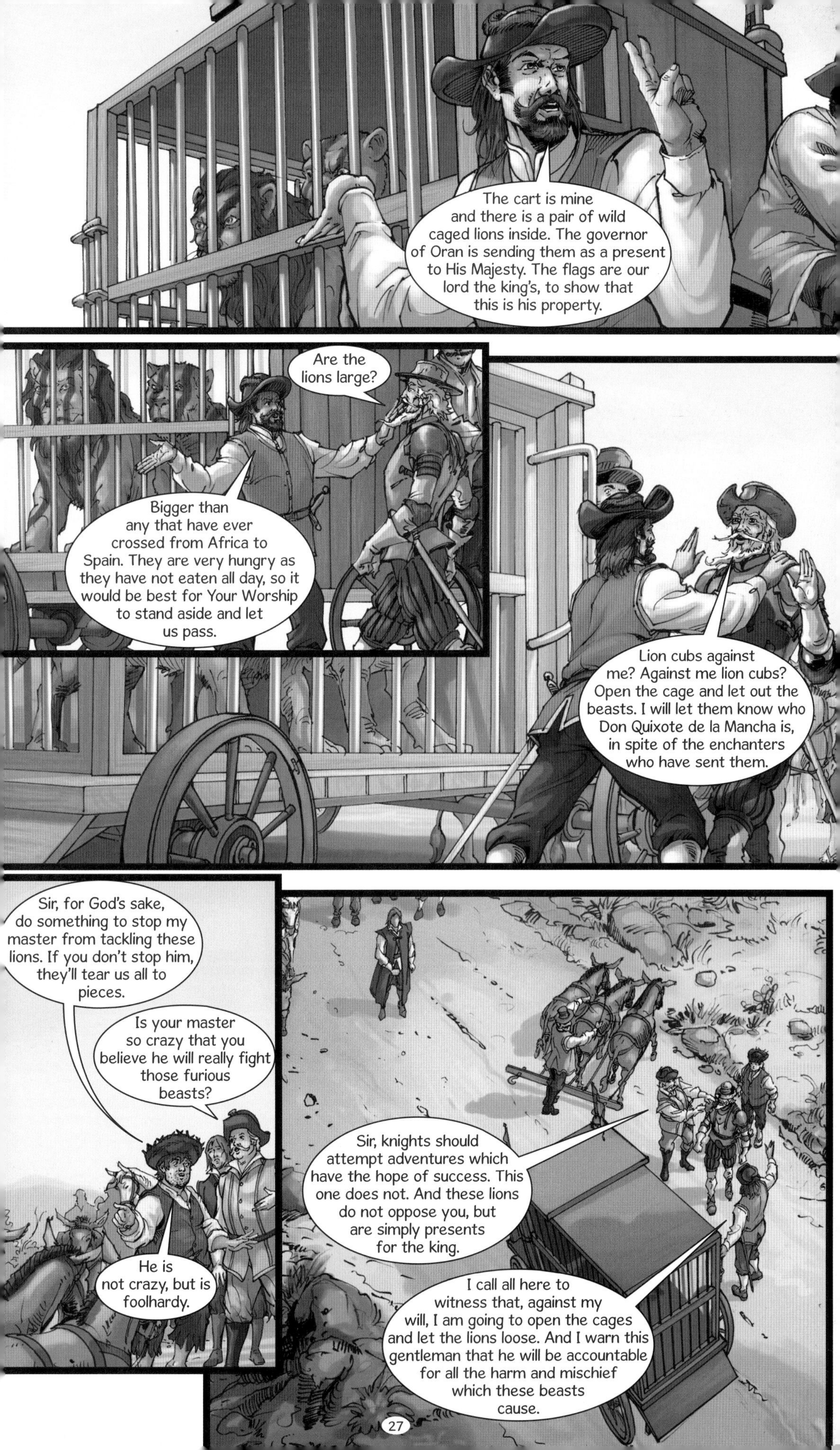
The cart is mine and there is a pair of wild caged lions inside. The governor of Oran is sending them as a present to His Majesty. The flags are our lord the king's, to show that this is his property.
Are the lions large?
Bigger than any that have ever crossed from Africa to Spain. They are very hungry as they have not eaten all day, so it would be best for Your Worship to stand aside and let us pass.
Lion cubs against me? Against me lion cubs? Open the cage and let out the beasts. I will let them know who Don Quixote de la Mancha is, in spite of the enchanters who have sent them.
Sir, for God's sake, do something to stop my master from tackling these lions. If you don't stop him, they'll tear us all to pieces.
Is your master so crazy that you believe he will really fight those furious beasts?
He is not crazy, but is foolhardy.
Sir, knights should attempt adventures which have the hope of success. This one does not. And these lions do not oppose you, but are simply presents for the king.
I call all here to witness that, against my will, I am going to open the cages and let the lions loose. And I warn this gentleman that he will be accountable for all the harm and mischief which these beasts cause.

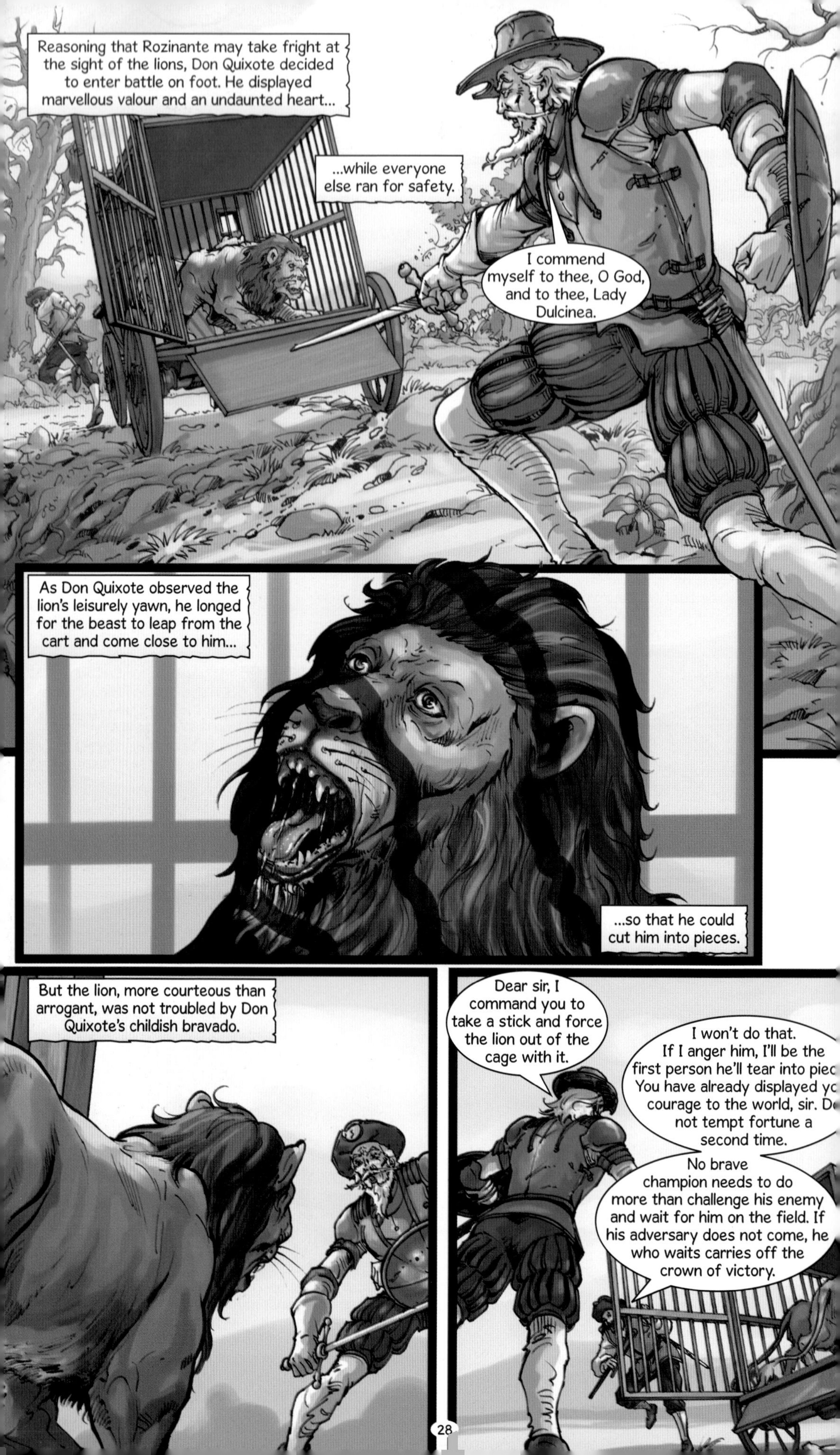

Reasoning that Rozinante may take fright at the sight of the lions, Don Quixote decided to enter battle on foot. He displayed marvellous valour and an undaunted heart...
...while everyone else ran for safety.
I commend myself to thee, O God, and to thee, Lady Dulcinea.
As Don Quixote observed the lion's leisurely yawn, he longed for the beast to leap from the cart and come close to him...
...so that he could cut him into pieces.
But the lion, more courteous than arrogant, was not troubled by Don Quixote's childish bravado.
Dear sir, I command you to take a stick and force the lion out of the cage with it.
I won't do that. If I anger him, I'll be the first person he'll tear into piec You have already displayed yo courage to the world, sir. Do not tempt fortune a second time.
No brave champion needs to do more than challenge his enemy and wait for him on the field. If his adversary does not come, he who waits carries off the crown of victory.

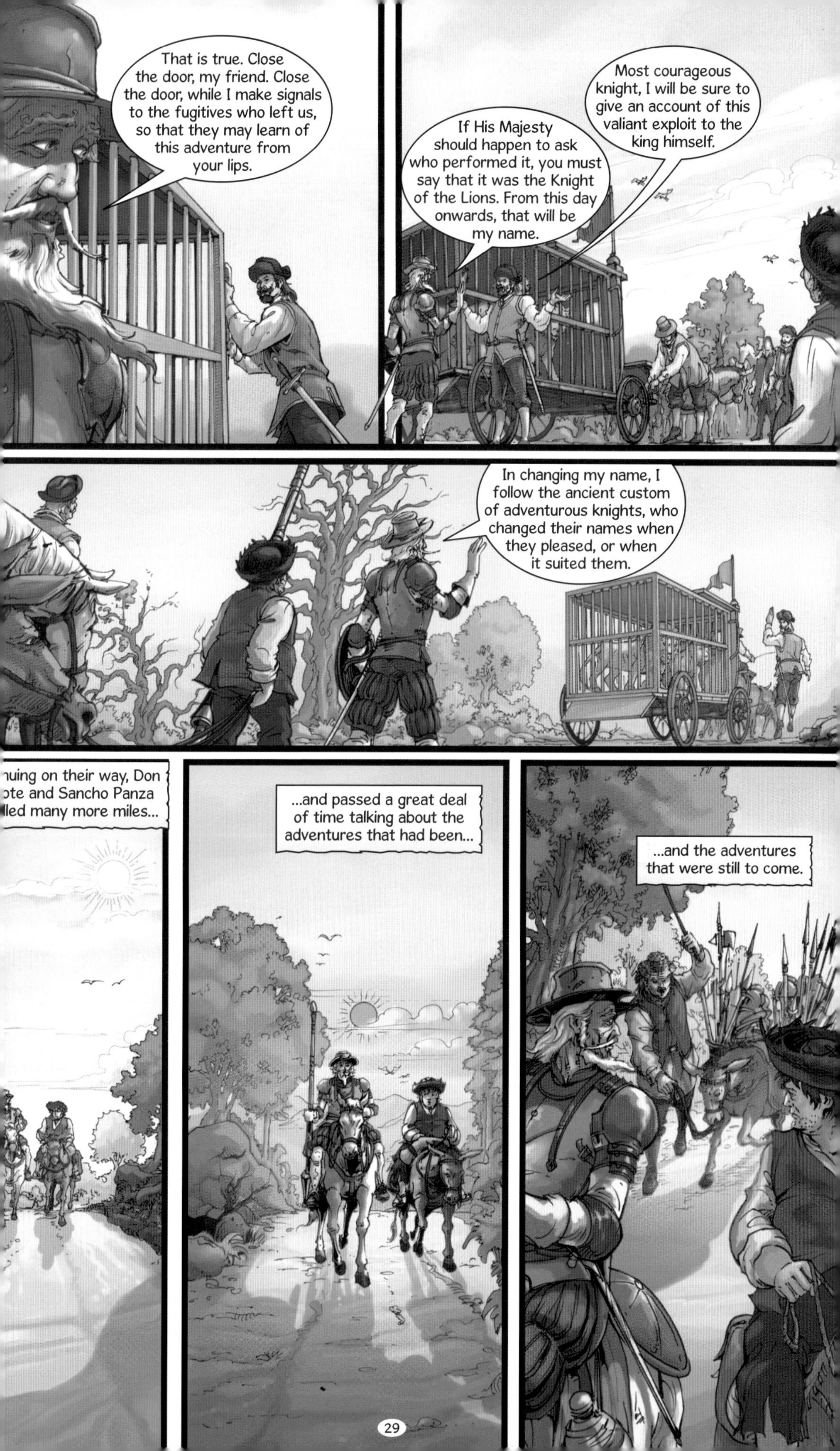
That is true. Close the door, my friend. Close the door, while I make signals to the fugitives who left us, so that they may learn of this adventure from your lips.
If His Majesty should happen to ask who performed it, you must say that it was the Knight of the Lions. From this day onwards, that will be my name.
Most courageous knight, I will be sure to give an account of this valiant exploit to the king himself.
In changing my name, I follow the ancient custom of adventurous knights, who changed their names when they pleased, or when it suited them.
uing on their way, Don
ote and Sancho Panza
lled many more miles...
...and passed a great deal of time talking about the adventures that had been...
...and the adventures that were still to come.

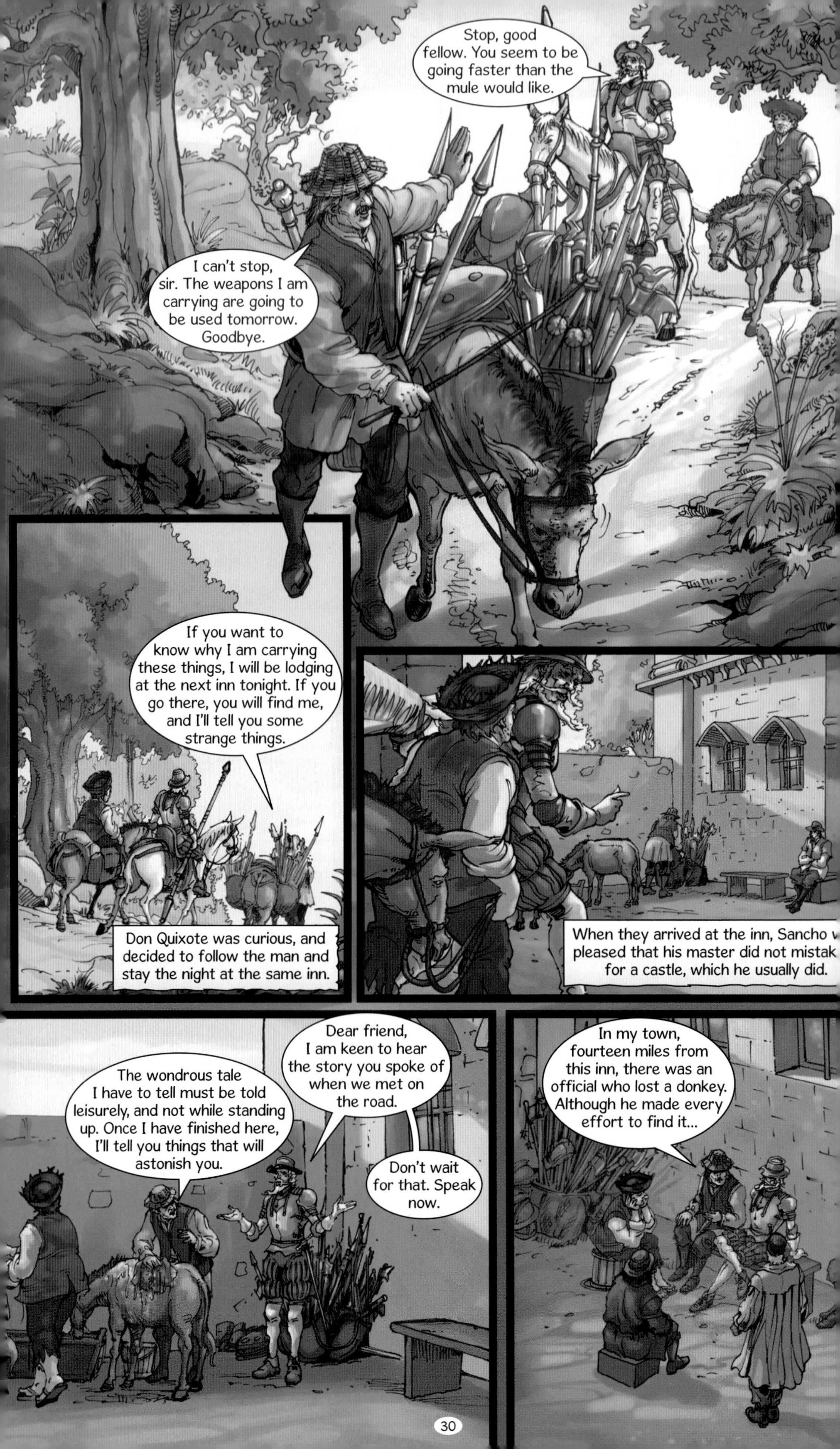

Stop, good fellow. You seem to be going faster than the mule would like.
I can't stop, sir. The weapons I am carrying are going to be used tomorrow. Goodbye.
If you want to know why I am carrying these things, I will be lodging at the next inn tonight. If you go there, you will find me, and I'll tell you some strange things.
Don Quixote was curious, and decided to follow the man and stay the night at the same inn.
When they arrived at the inn, Sancho
pleased that his master did not mistak
for a castle, which he usually did.
Dear friend, I am keen to hear the story you spoke of when we met on the road.
The wondrous tale I have to tell must be told leisurely, and not while standing up. Once I have finished here, I'll tell you things that will astonish you.
Don't wait for that. Speak now.
In my town, fourteen miles from this inn, there was an official who lost a donkey. Although he made every effort to find it...

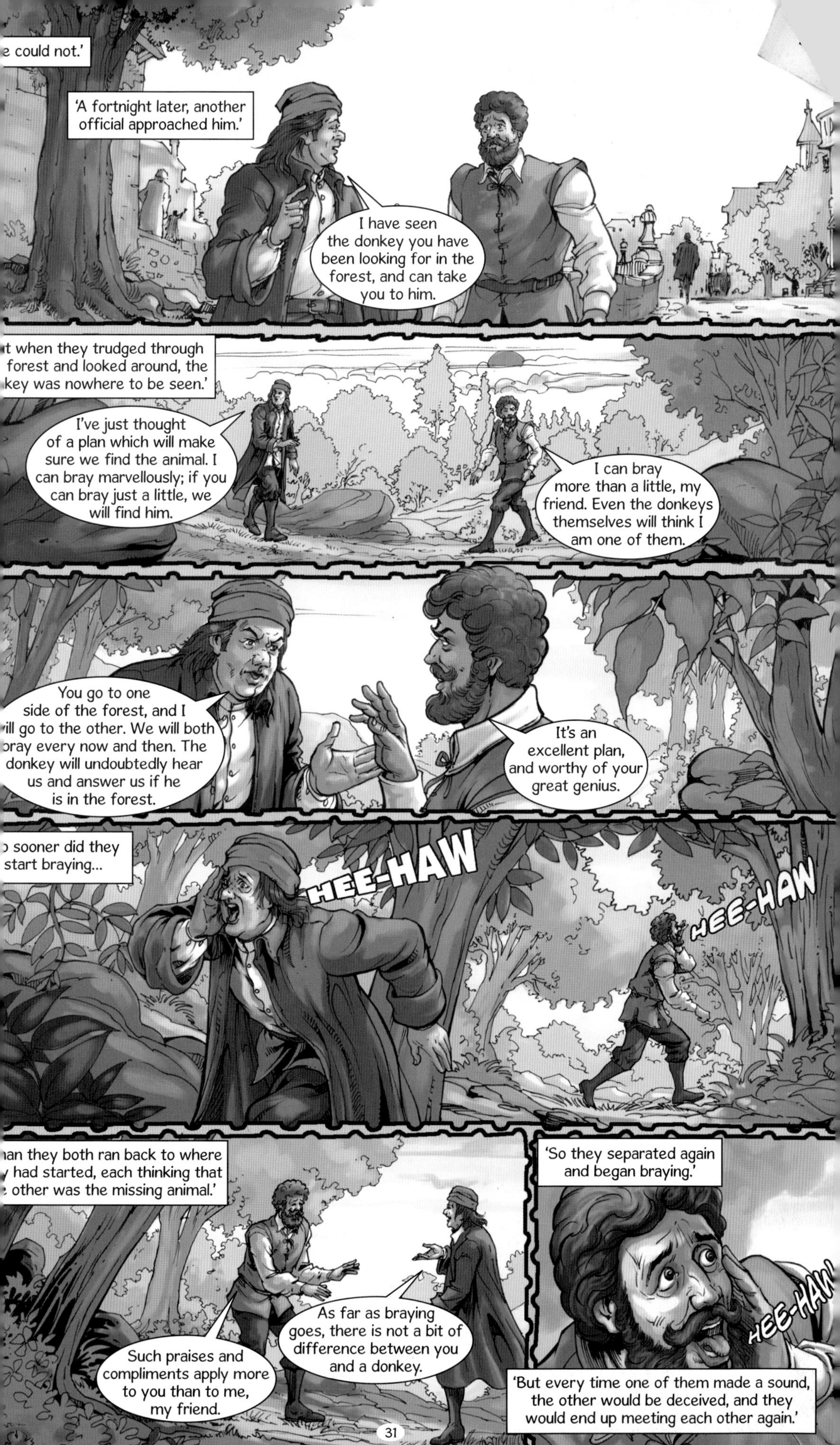

e could not.'
'A fortnight later, another official approached him.'
I have seen the donkey you have been looking for in the forest, and can take you to him.
t when they trudged through forest and looked around, the key was nowhere to be seen.'
I've just thought of a plan which will make sure we find the animal. I can bray marvellously; if you can bray just a little, we will find him.
I can bray more than a little, my friend. Even the donkeys themselves will think I am one of them.
You go to one side of the forest, and I ill go to the other. We will both bray every now and then. The donkey will undoubtedly hear us and answer us if he is in the forest.
It's an excellent plan, and worthy of your great genius.
sooner did they start braying...
HEE-HAW
HEE-HAW
an they both ran back to where had started, each thinking that other was the missing animal.'
As far as braying goes, there is not a bit of difference between you and a donkey.
Such praises and compliments apply more to you than to me, my friend.
'So they separated again and began braying.'
HEE-HAW
'But every time one of them made a sound, the other would be deceived, and they would end up meeting each other again.'

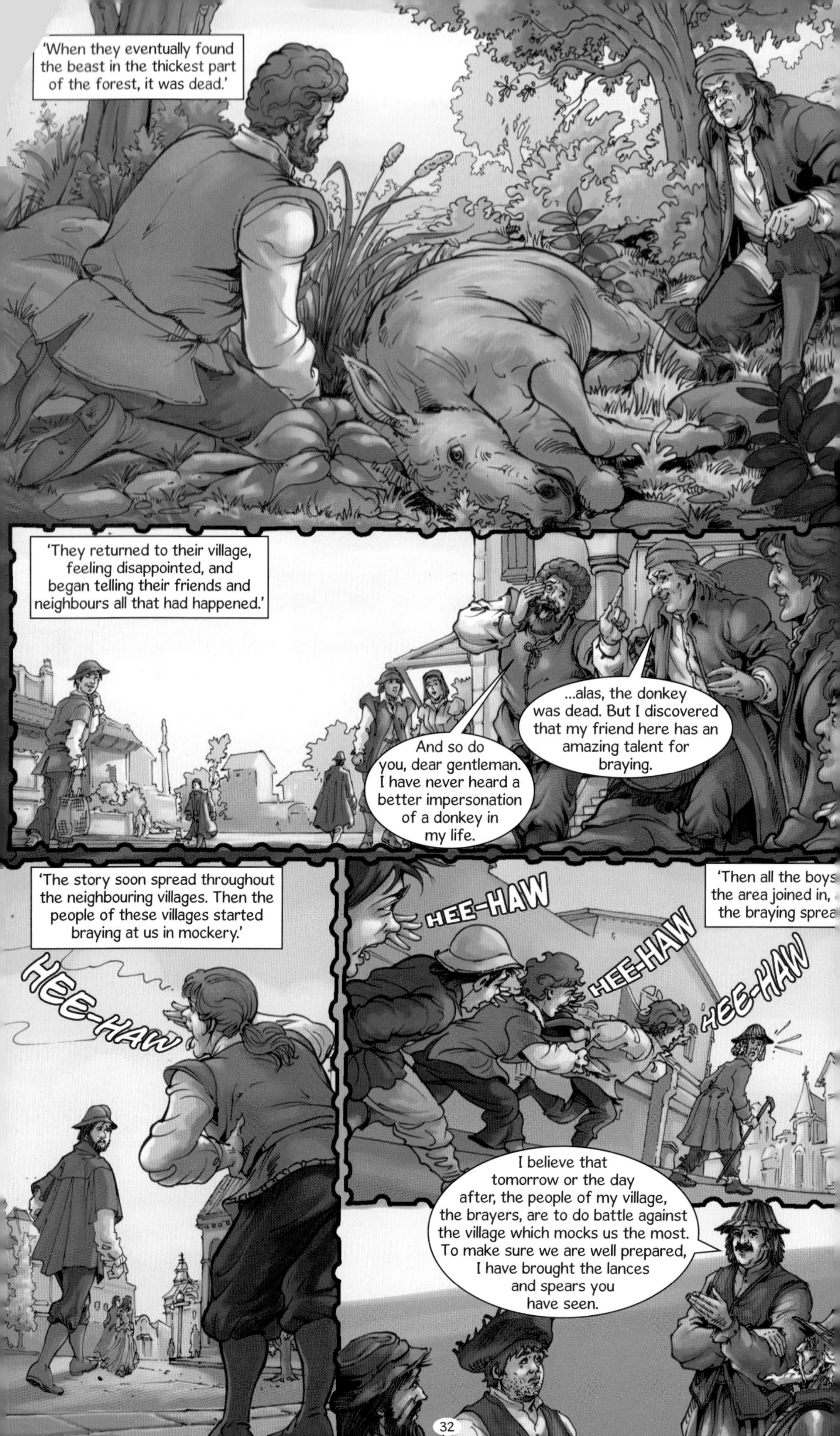
'When they eventually found the beast in the thickest part of the forest, it was dead.'
'They returned to their village, feeling disappointed, and began telling their friends and neighbours all that had happened.'
...alas, the donkey was dead. But I discovered that my friend here has an amazing talent for braying.
And so do you, dear gentleman. I have never heard a better impersonation of a donkey in my life.
'The story soon spread throughout the neighbouring villages. Then the people of these villages started braying at us in mockery.'
HEE-HAW
'Then all the boys the area joined in, the braying sprea
HEE-HAW
HEE-HAW
HEE-HAW
I believe that tomorrow or the day after, the people of my village, the brayers, are to do battle against the village which mocks us the most. To make sure we are well prepared, I have brought the lances and spears you have seen.

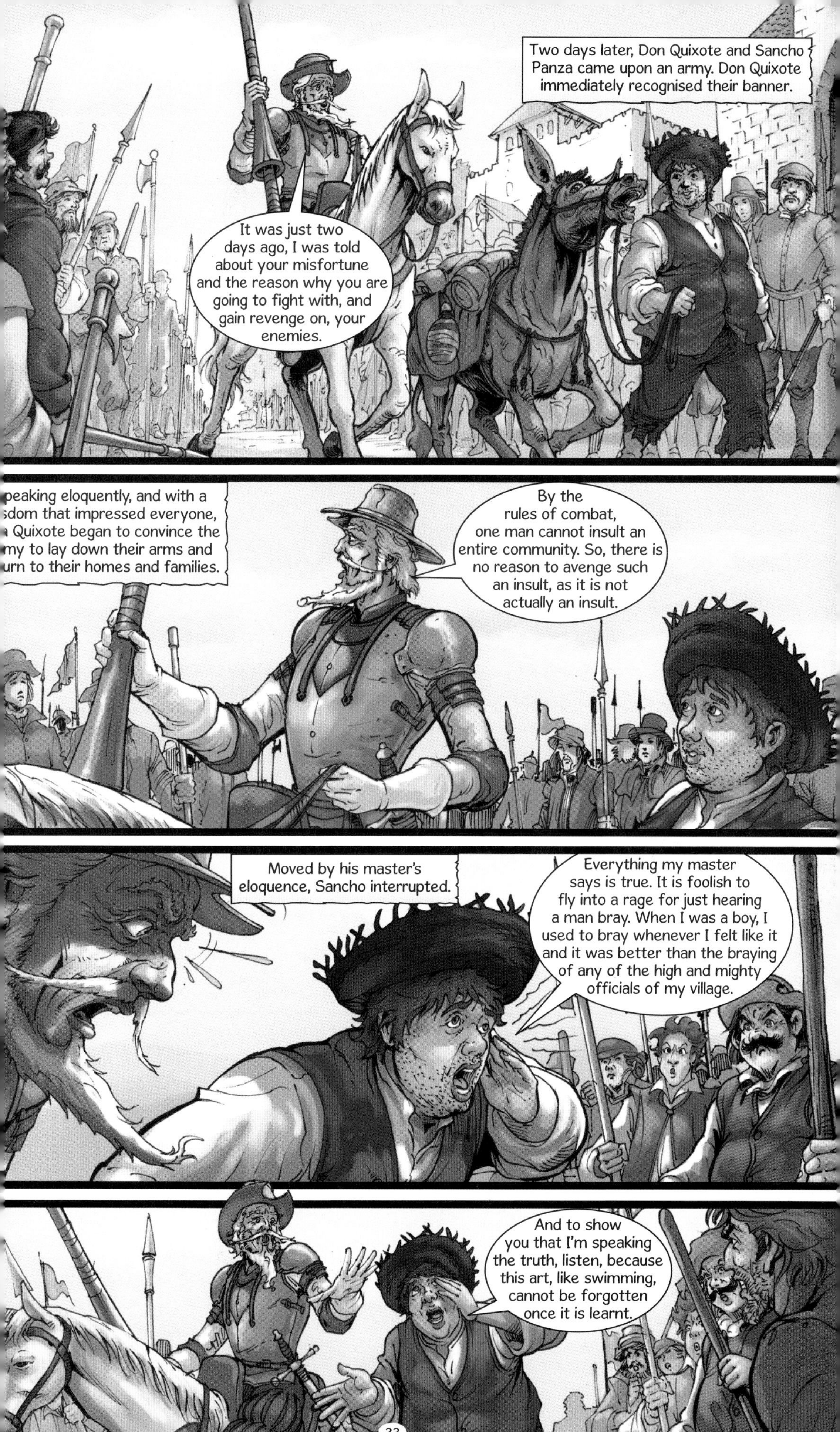
Two days later, Don Quixote and Sancho Panza came upon an army. Don Quixote immediately recognised their banner.
It was just two days ago, I was told about your misfortune and the reason why you are going to fight with, and gain revenge on, your enemies.
peaking eloquently, and with a sdom that impressed everyone, Quixote began to convince the my to lay down their arms and urn to their homes and families.
By the rules of combat, one man cannot insult an entire community. So, there is no reason to avenge such an insult, as it is not actually an insult.
Moved by his master's eloquence, Sancho interrupted.
Everything my master says is true. It is foolish to fly into a rage for just hearing a man bray. When I was a boy, I used to bray whenever I felt like it and it was better than the braying of any of the high and mighty officials of my village.
And to show you that I'm speaking the truth, listen, because this art, like swimming, cannot be forgotten once it is learnt.

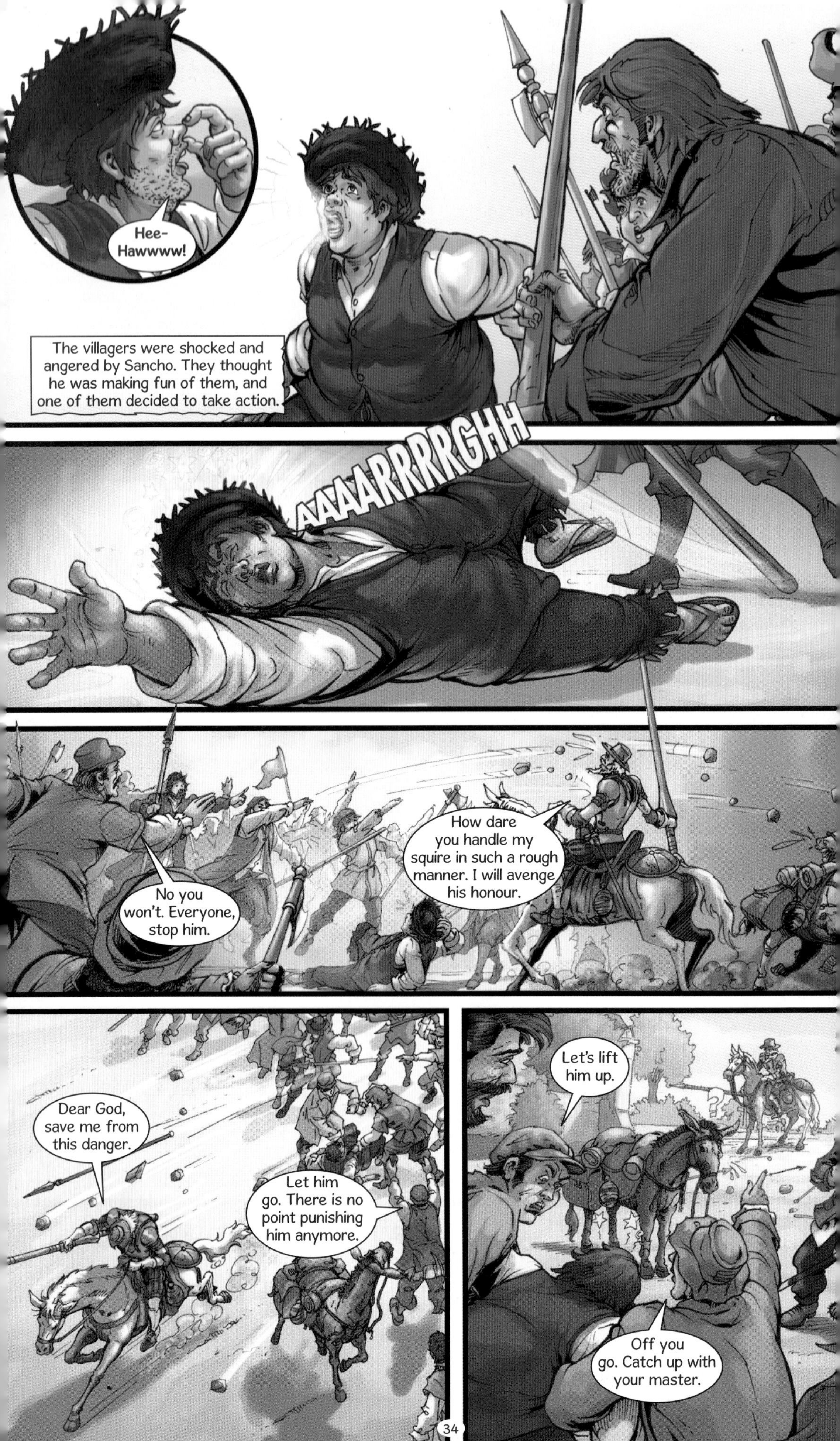
Hee-Hawwww!
The villagers were shocked and angered by Sancho. They thought he was making fun of them, and one of them decided to take action.
AAAARRRRGHH
How dare you handle my squire in such a rough manner. I will avenge his honour.
No you won't. Everyone, stop him.
Dear God, save me from this danger.
Let him go. There is no point punishing him anymore.
Let's lift him up.
Off you go. Catch up with your master.

At such an important moment, why did you decide to start braying, Sancho? What made you think it was a good idea to mention rope in the house of a man who has been hanged?

I can't answer that, as I feel terrible. Let us get away from this place.

I won't bray anymore, but I'll say that valorous knights run away and leave their squires to be beaten up at the hands of their enemies.

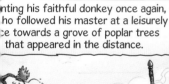

...nting his faithful donkey once again, ...ho followed his master at a leisurely ...ce towards a grove of poplar trees that appeared in the distance.

With each passing ..., oh Master, I discover ...e and more what little ...pe I have by staying in your company.

Talk away, my son. Say whatever comes into your head, because while you are talking I'm sure you feel no pain.

And while you feel no pain, the irritation of your disrespectful comments will be a pleasure to me.

When I worked for Thomas Carrasco, the father of Samson Carrasco, I used to earn two ducats a month besides my food.

I don't know what I will earn with Your Worship, but I know that a knight's squire works harder than a farmer.

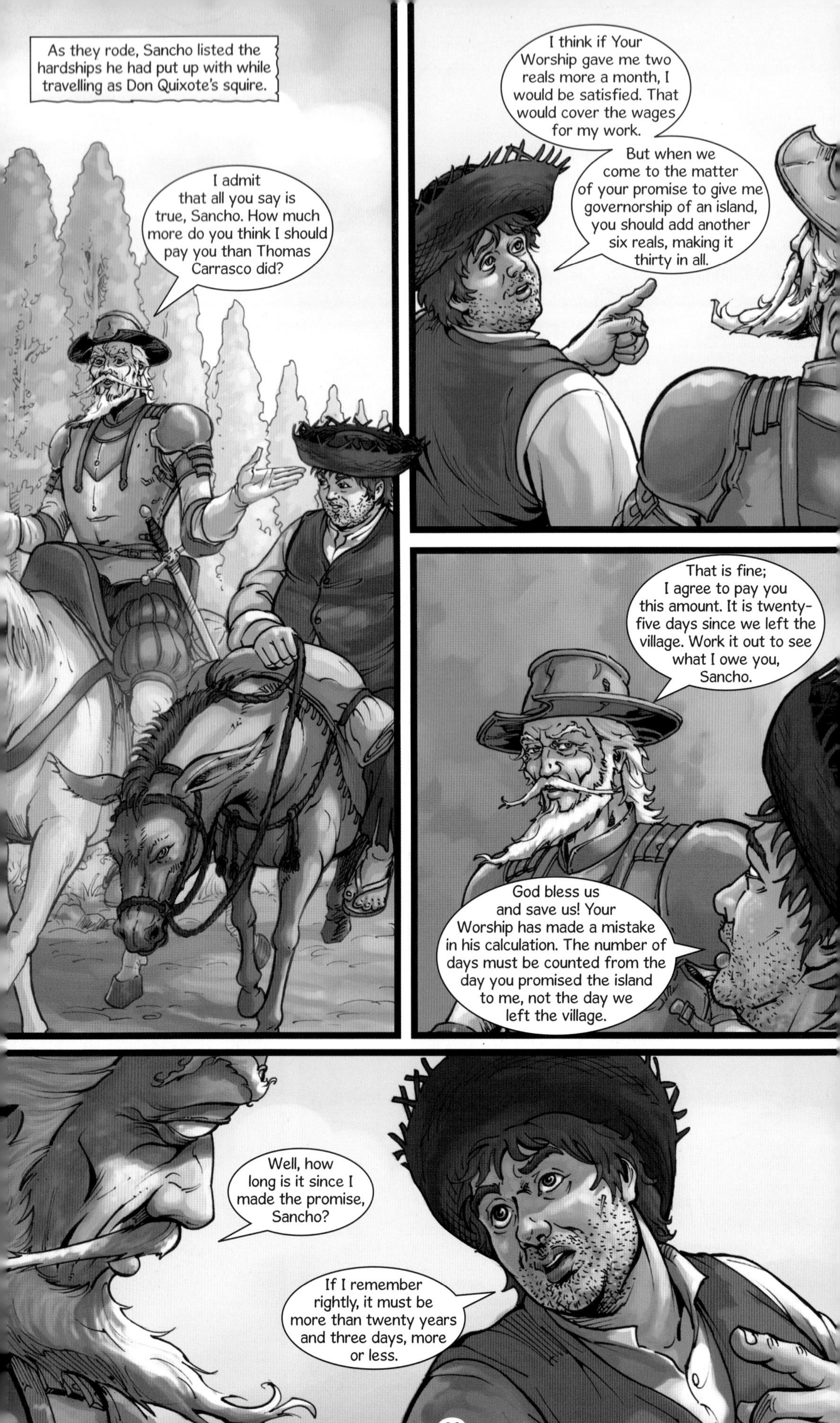
As they rode, Sancho listed the hardships he had put up with while travelling as Don Quixote's squire.
I admit that all you say is true, Sancho. How much more do you think I should pay you than Thomas Carrasco did?
I think if Your Worship gave me two reals more a month, I would be satisfied. That would cover the wages for my work.
But when we come to the matter of your promise to give me governorship of an island, you should add another six reals, making it thirty in all.
That is fine; I agree to pay you this amount. It is twenty-five days since we left the village. Work it out to see what I owe you, Sancho.
God bless us and save us! Your Worship has made a mistake in his calculation. The number of days must be counted from the day you promised the island to me, not the day we left the village.
Well, how long is it since I made the promise, Sancho?
If I remember rightly, it must be more than twenty years and three days, more or less.

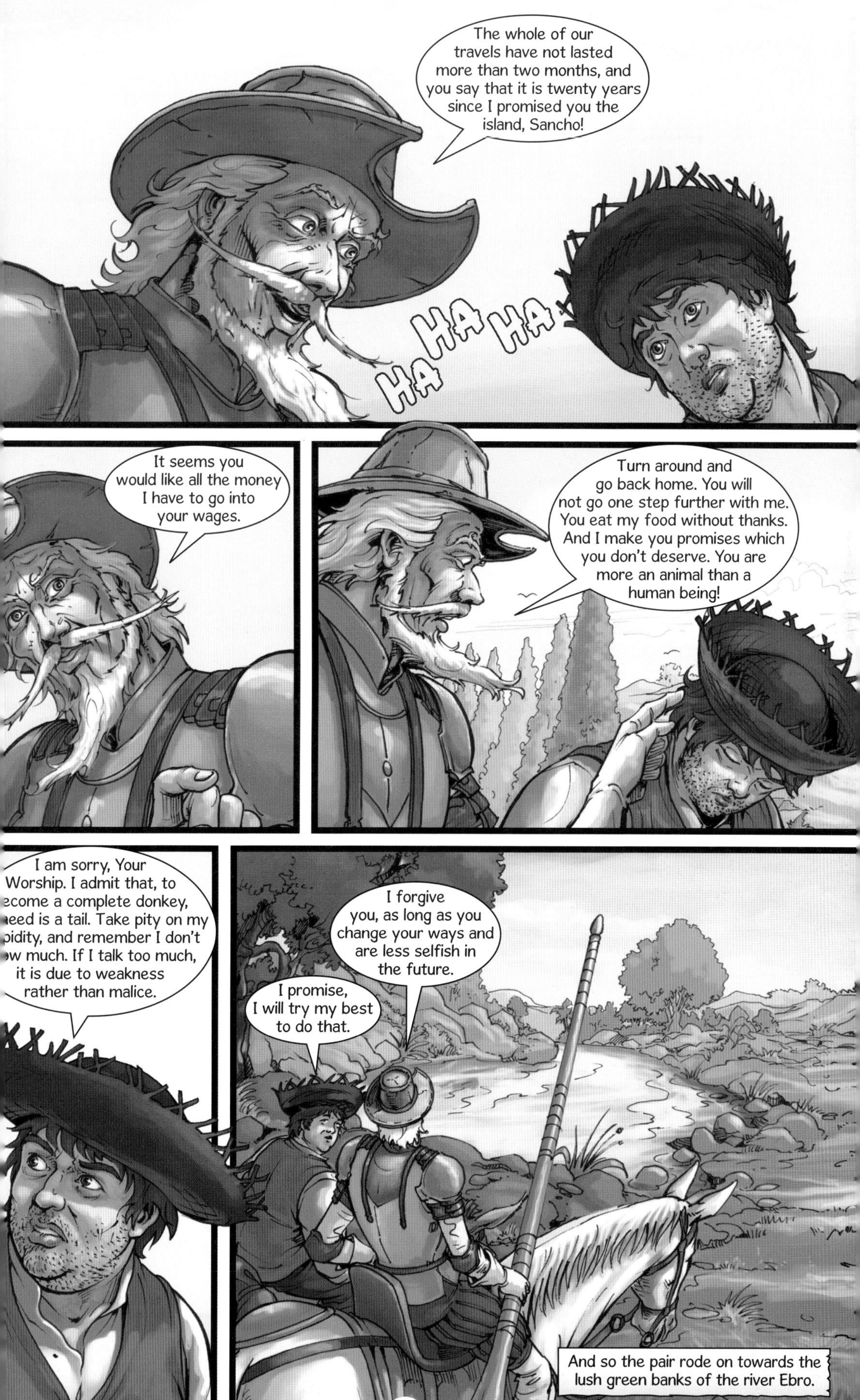
The whole of our travels have not lasted more than two months, and you say that it is twenty years since I promised you the island, Sancho!
HA HA HA
It seems you would like all the money I have to go into your wages.
Turn around and go back home. You will not go one step further with me. You eat my food without thanks. And I make you promises which you don't deserve. You are more an animal than a human being!
I am sorry, Your Worship. I admit that, to ecome a complete donkey, eed is a tail. Take pity on my pidity, and remember I don't w much. If I talk too much, it is due to weakness rather than malice.
I forgive you, as long as you change your ways and are less selfish in the future.
I promise, I will try my best to do that.
And so the pair rode on towards the lush green banks of the river Ebro.

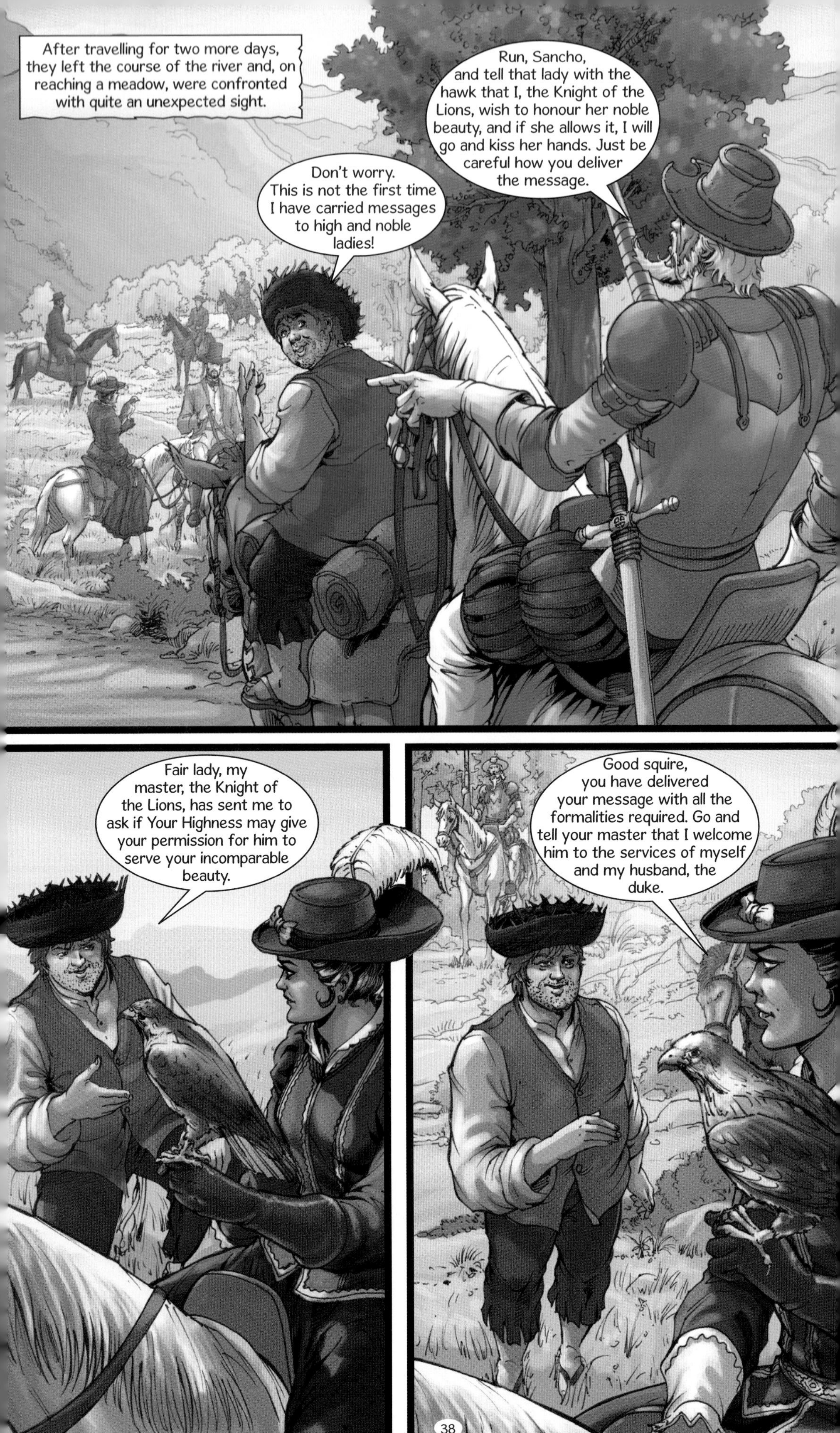

After travelling for two more days, they left the course of the river and, on reaching a meadow, were confronted with quite an unexpected sight.
Run, Sancho, and tell that lady with the hawk that I, the Knight of the Lions, wish to honour her noble beauty, and if she allows it, I will go and kiss her hands. Just be careful how you deliver the message.
Don't worry. This is not the first time I have carried messages to high and noble ladies!
Fair lady, my master, the Knight of the Lions, has sent me to ask if Your Highness may give your permission for him to serve your incomparable beauty.
Good squire, you have delivered your message with all the formalities required. Go and tell your master that I welcome him to the services of myself and my husband, the duke.

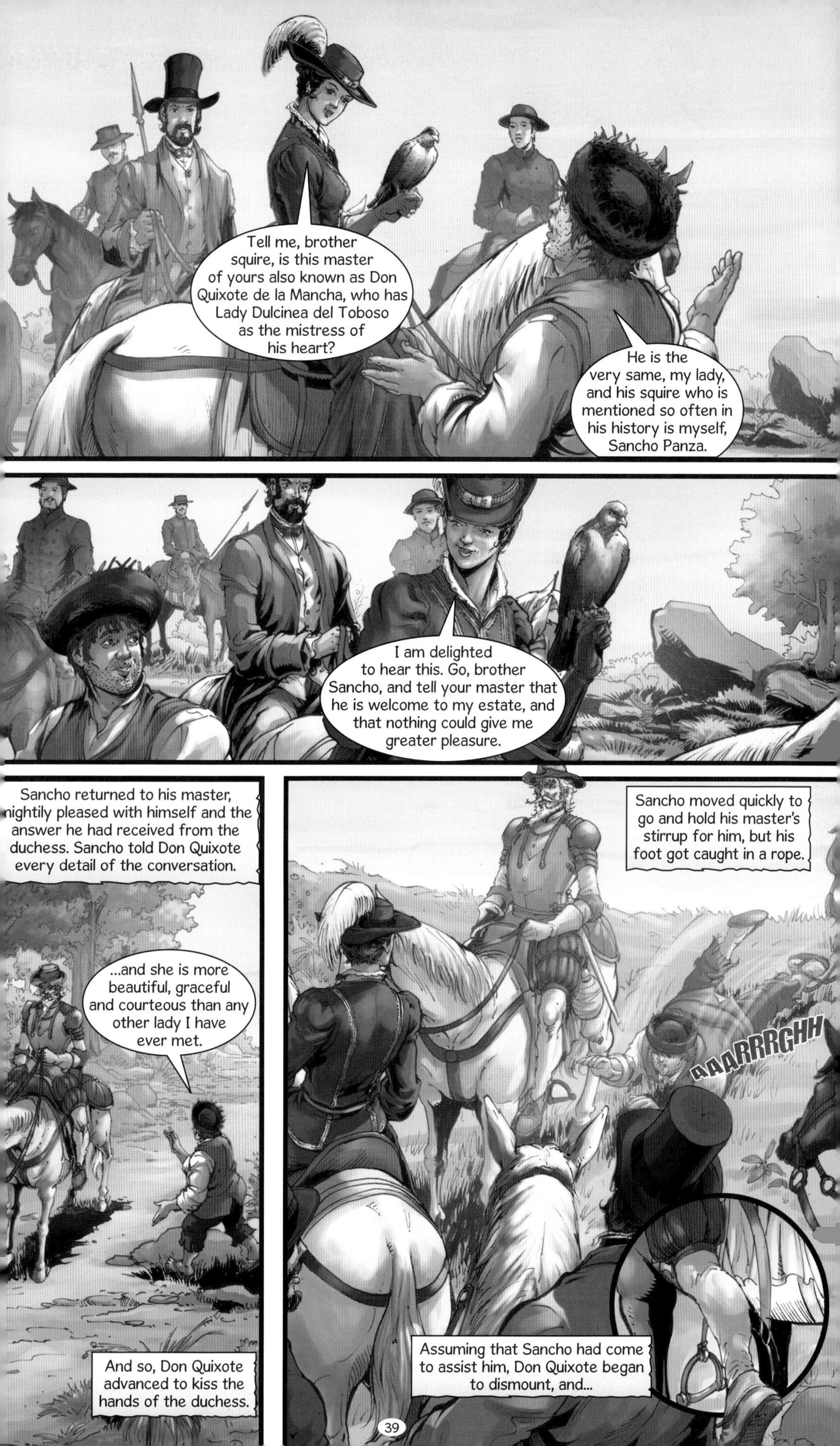

Tell me, brother squire, is this master of yours also known as Don Quixote de la Mancha, who has Lady Dulcinea del Toboso as the mistress of his heart?
He is the very same, my lady, and his squire who is mentioned so often in his history is myself, Sancho Panza.
I am delighted to hear this. Go, brother Sancho, and tell your master that he is welcome to my estate, and that nothing could give me greater pleasure.
Sancho returned to his master, nightily pleased with himself and the answer he had received from the duchess. Sancho told Don Quixote every detail of the conversation.
...and she is more beautiful, graceful and courteous than any other lady I have ever met.
And so, Don Quixote advanced to kiss the hands of the duchess.
Sancho moved quickly to go and hold his master's stirrup for him, but his foot got caught in a rope.
AAARRRGHH
Assuming that Sancho had come to assist him, Don Quixote began to dismount, and...

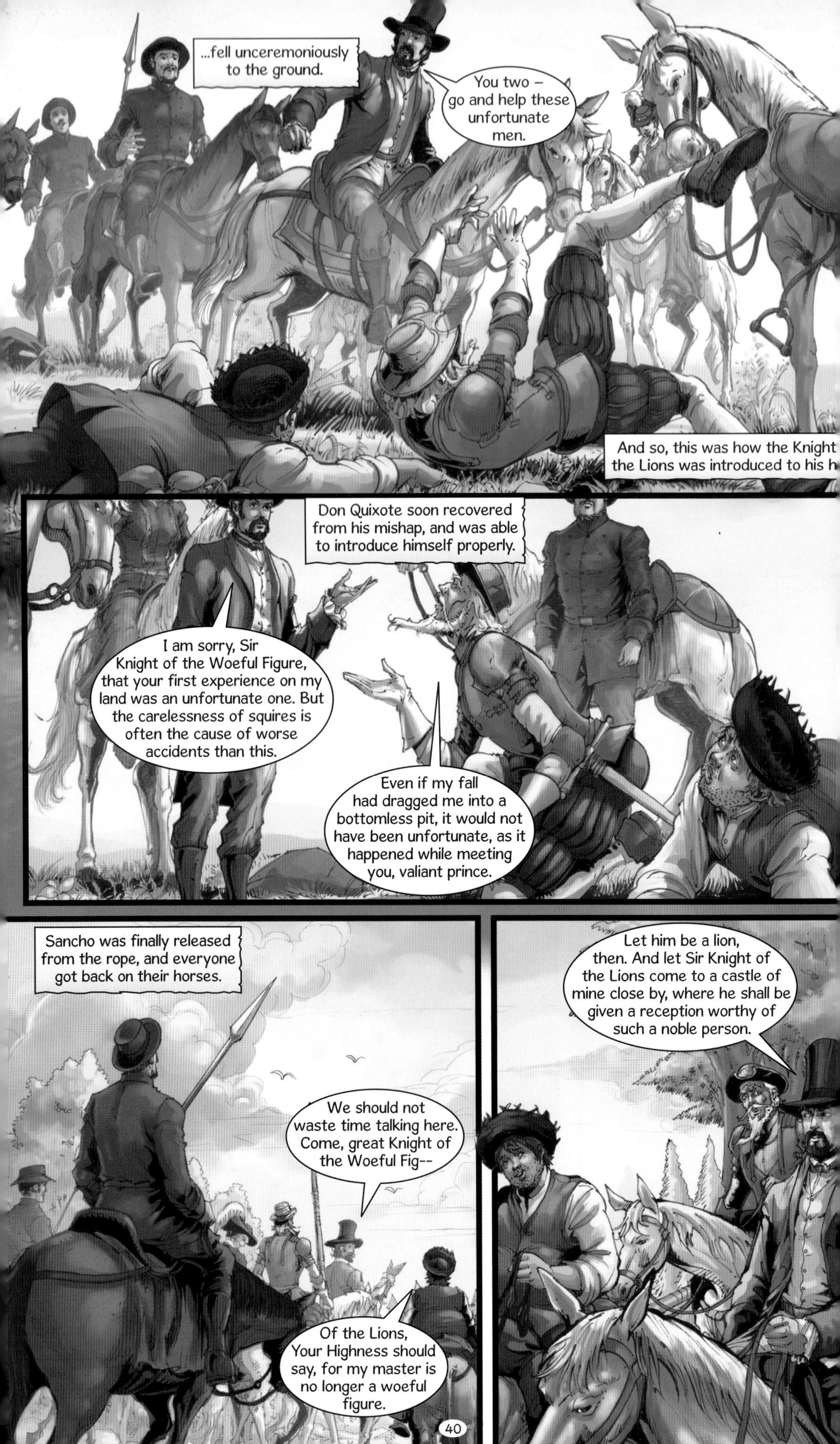
...fell unceremoniously to the ground.
You two – go and help these unfortunate men.
And so, this was how the Knight of the Lions was introduced to his h
Don Quixote soon recovered from his mishap, and was able to introduce himself properly.
I am sorry, Sir Knight of the Woeful Figure, that your first experience on my land was an unfortunate one. But the carelessness of squires is often the cause of worse accidents than this.
Even if my fall had dragged me into a bottomless pit, it would not have been unfortunate, as it happened while meeting you, valiant prince.
Sancho was finally released from the rope, and everyone got back on their horses.
We should not waste time talking here. Come, great Knight of the Woeful Fig--
Of the Lions, Your Highness should say, for my master is no longer a woeful figure.
Let him be a lion, then. And let Sir Knight of the Lions come to a castle of mine close by, where he shall be given a reception worthy of such a noble person.

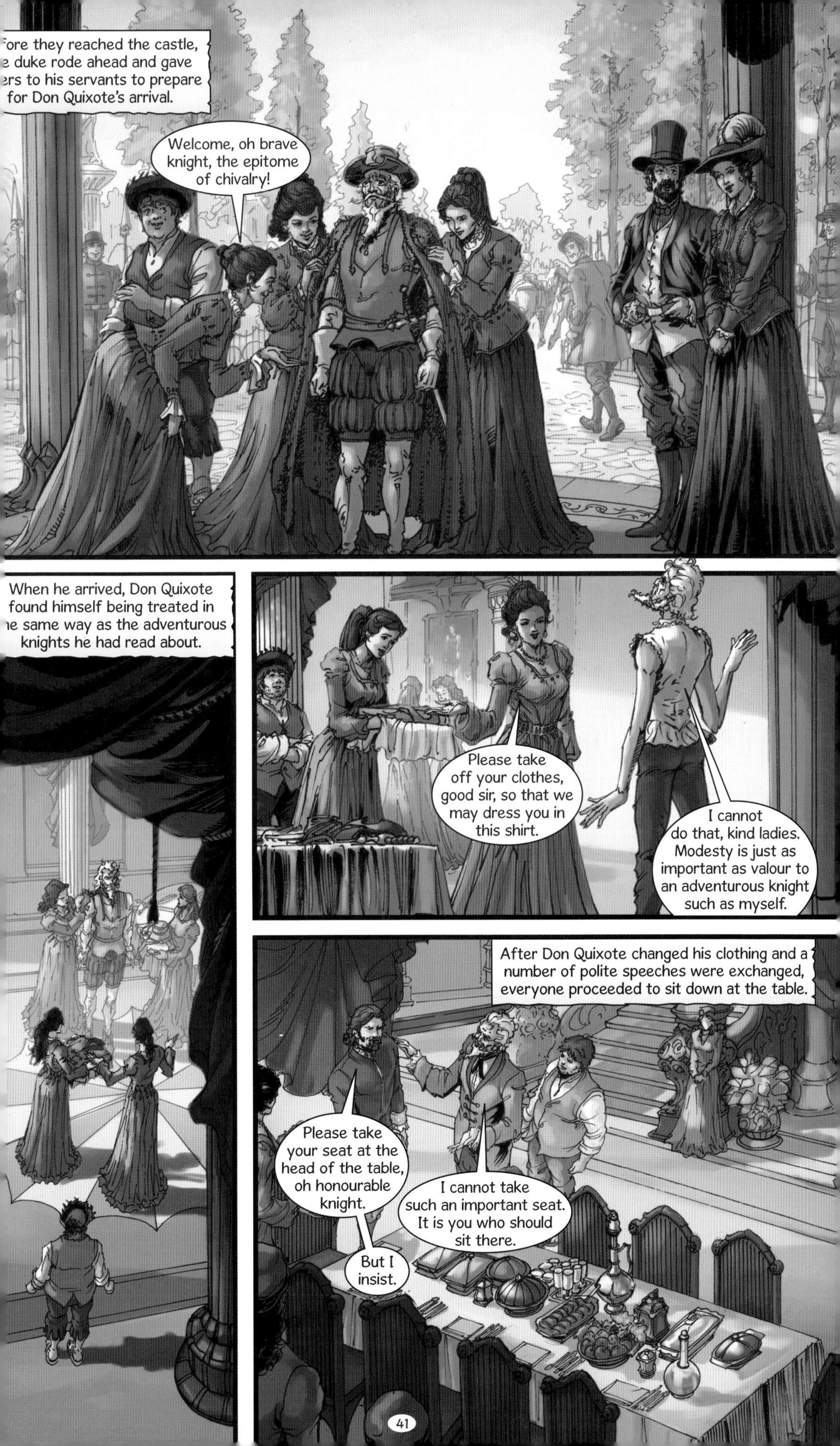

fore they reached the castle, e duke rode ahead and gave ers to his servants to prepare for Don Quixote's arrival.
Welcome, oh brave knight, the epitome of chivalry!
When he arrived, Don Quixote found himself being treated in e same way as the adventurous knights he had read about.
Please take off your clothes, good sir, so that we may dress you in this shirt.
I cannot do that, kind ladies. Modesty is just as important as valour to an adventurous knight such as myself.
After Don Quixote changed his clothing and a number of polite speeches were exchanged, everyone proceeded to sit down at the table.
Please take your seat at the head of the table, oh honourable knight.
I cannot take such an important seat. It is you who should sit there.
But I insist.

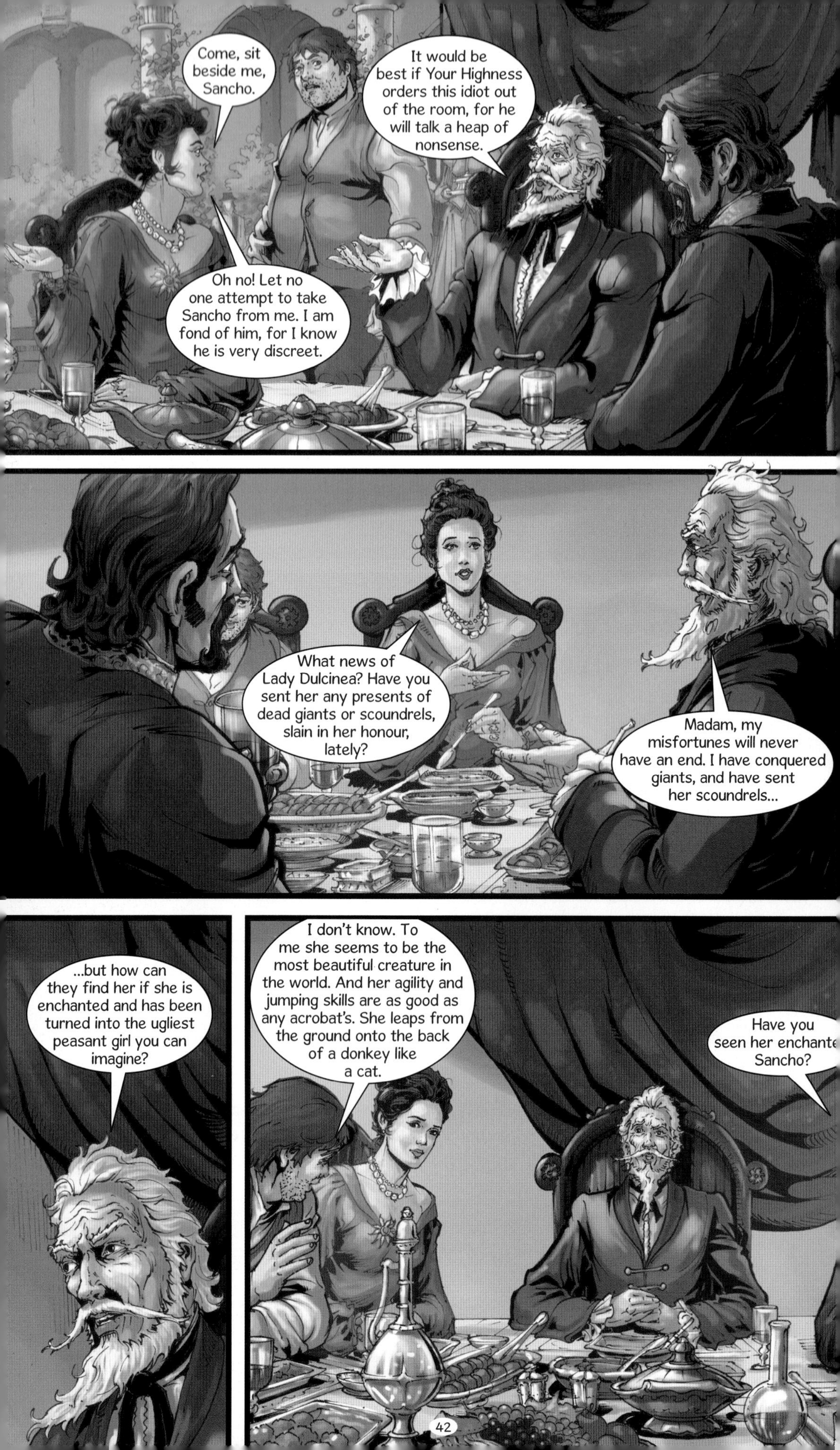
Come, sit beside me, Sancho.
It would be best if Your Highness orders this idiot out of the room, for he will talk a heap of nonsense.
Oh no! Let no one attempt to take Sancho from me. I am fond of him, for I know he is very discreet.
What news of Lady Dulcinea? Have you sent her any presents of dead giants or scoundrels, slain in her honour, lately?
Madam, my misfortunes will never have an end. I have conquered giants, and have sent her scoundrels...
...but how can they find her if she is enchanted and has been turned into the ugliest peasant girl you can imagine?
Have you seen her enchante
Sancho?
I don't know. To me she seems to be the most beautiful creature in the world. And her agility and jumping skills are as good as any acrobat's. She leaps from the ground onto the back of a donkey like a cat.

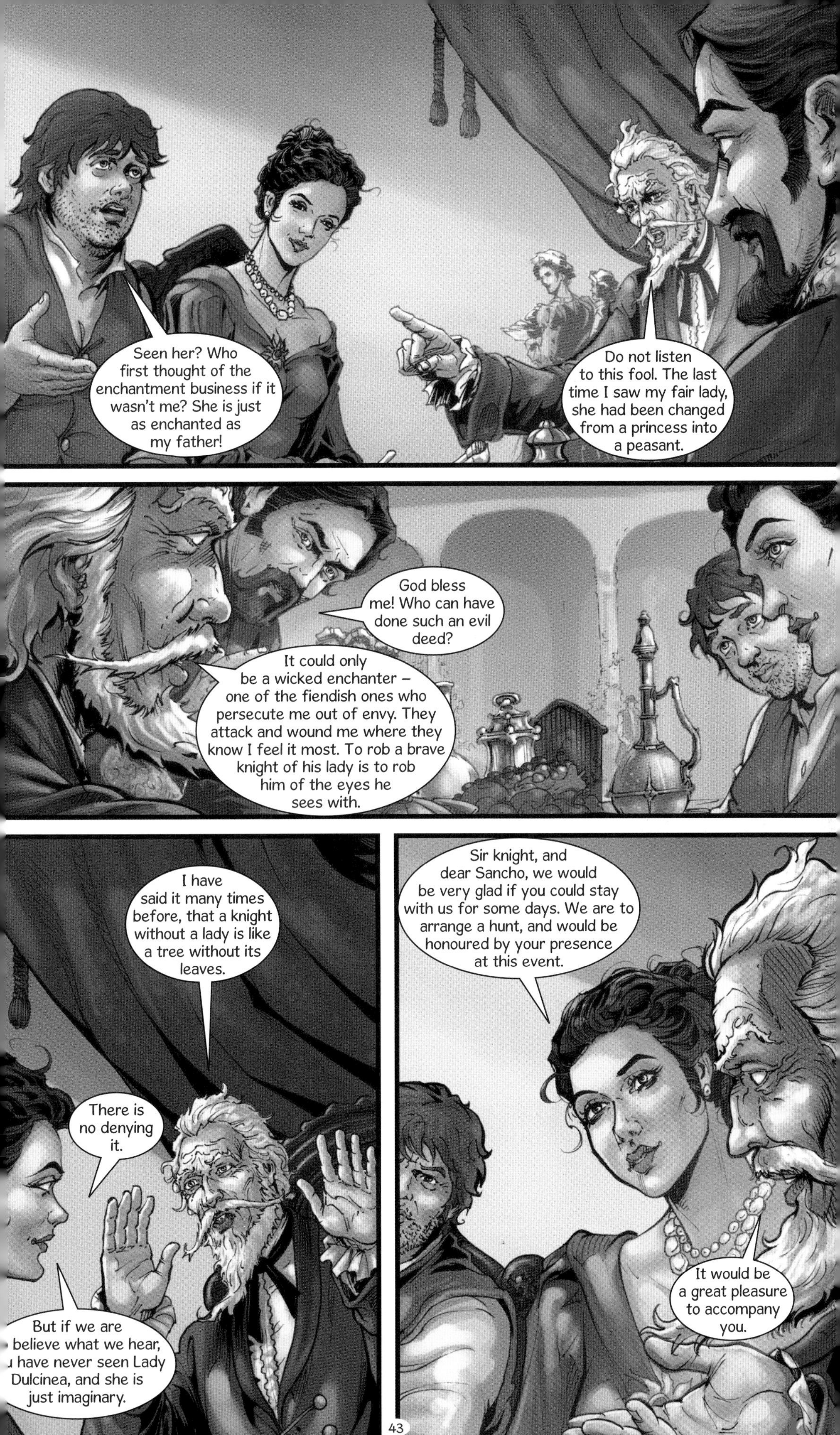
Seen her? Who first thought of the enchantment business if it wasn't me? She is just as enchanted as my father!
Do not listen to this fool. The last time I saw my fair lady, she had been changed from a princess into a peasant.
God bless me! Who can have done such an evil deed?
It could only be a wicked enchanter – one of the fiendish ones who persecute me out of envy. They attack and wound me where they know I feel it most. To rob a brave knight of his lady is to rob him of the eyes he sees with.
I have said it many times before, that a knight without a lady is like a tree without its leaves.
There is no denying it.
But if we are believe what we hear, u have never seen Lady Dulcinea, and she is just imaginary.
Sir knight, and dear Sancho, we would be very glad if you could stay with us for some days. We are to arrange a hunt, and would be honoured by your presence at this event.
It would be a great pleasure to accompany you.

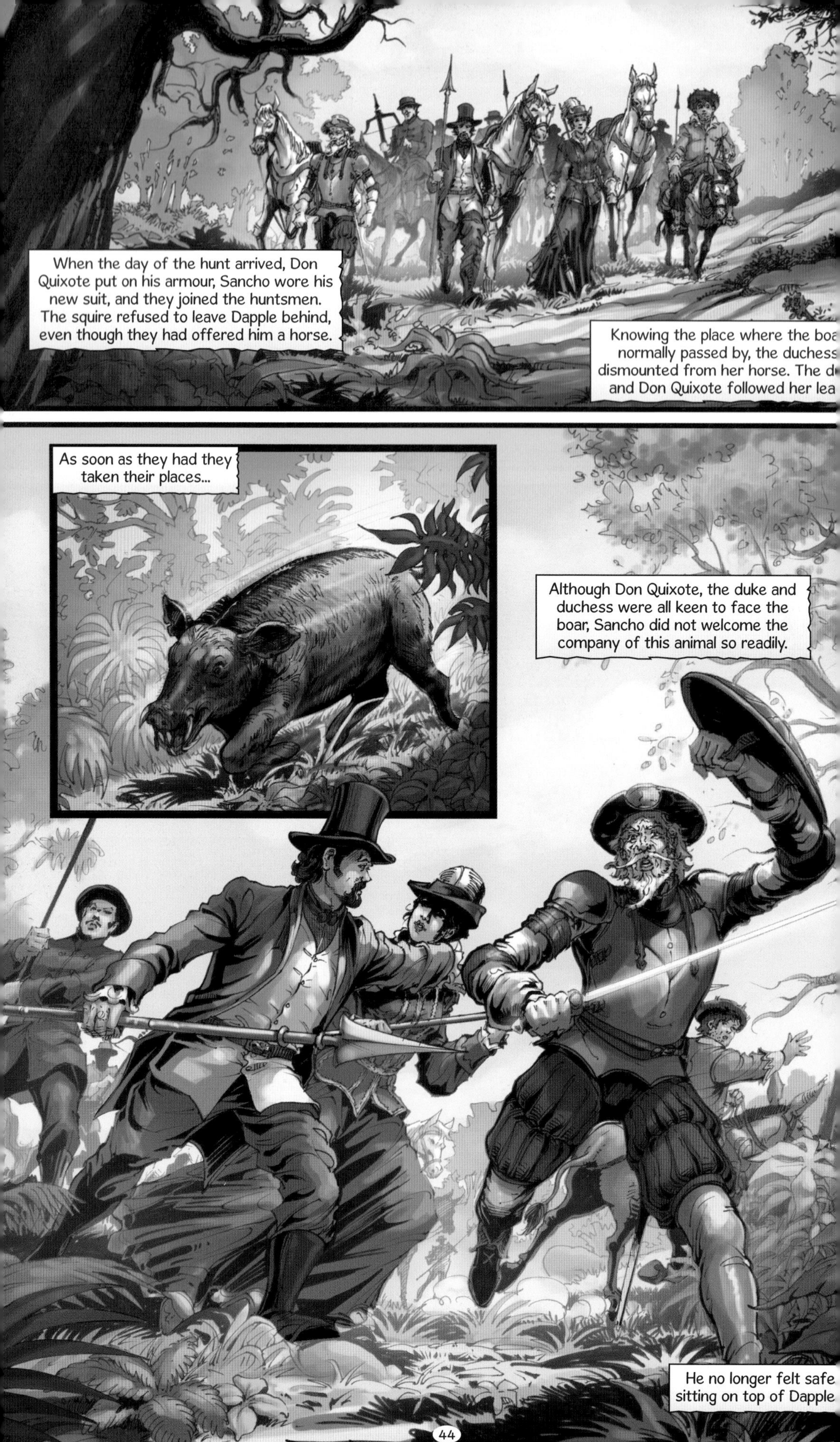
When the day of the hunt arrived, Don Quixote put on his armour, Sancho wore his new suit, and they joined the huntsmen. The squire refused to leave Dapple behind, even though they had offered him a horse.
Knowing the place where the boa normally passed by, the duchess dismounted from her horse. The d and Don Quixote followed her lea
As soon as they had they taken their places...
Although Don Quixote, the duke and duchess were all keen to face the boar, Sancho did not welcome the company of this animal so readily.
He no longer felt safe sitting on top of Dapple

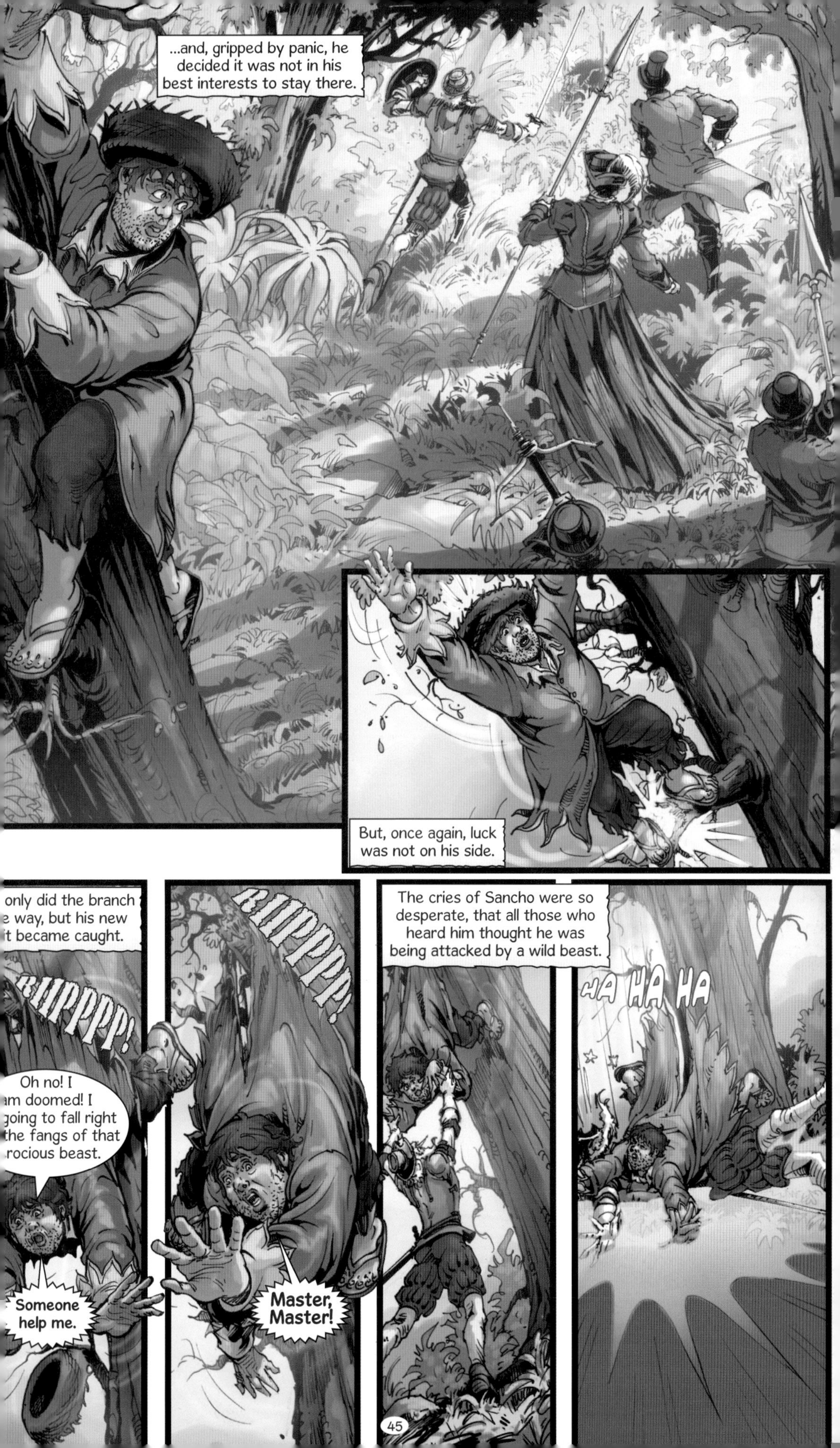
...and, gripped by panic, he decided it was not in his best interests to stay there.
But, once again, luck was not on his side.
only did the branch
e way, but his new
it became caught.
RIPPPPP!
Oh no! I
m doomed! I
going to fall right
the fangs of that
rocious beast.
Someone help me.
RIPPPPP!
Master, Master!
The cries of Sancho were so desperate, that all those who heard him thought he was being attacked by a wild beast.
HA HA HA

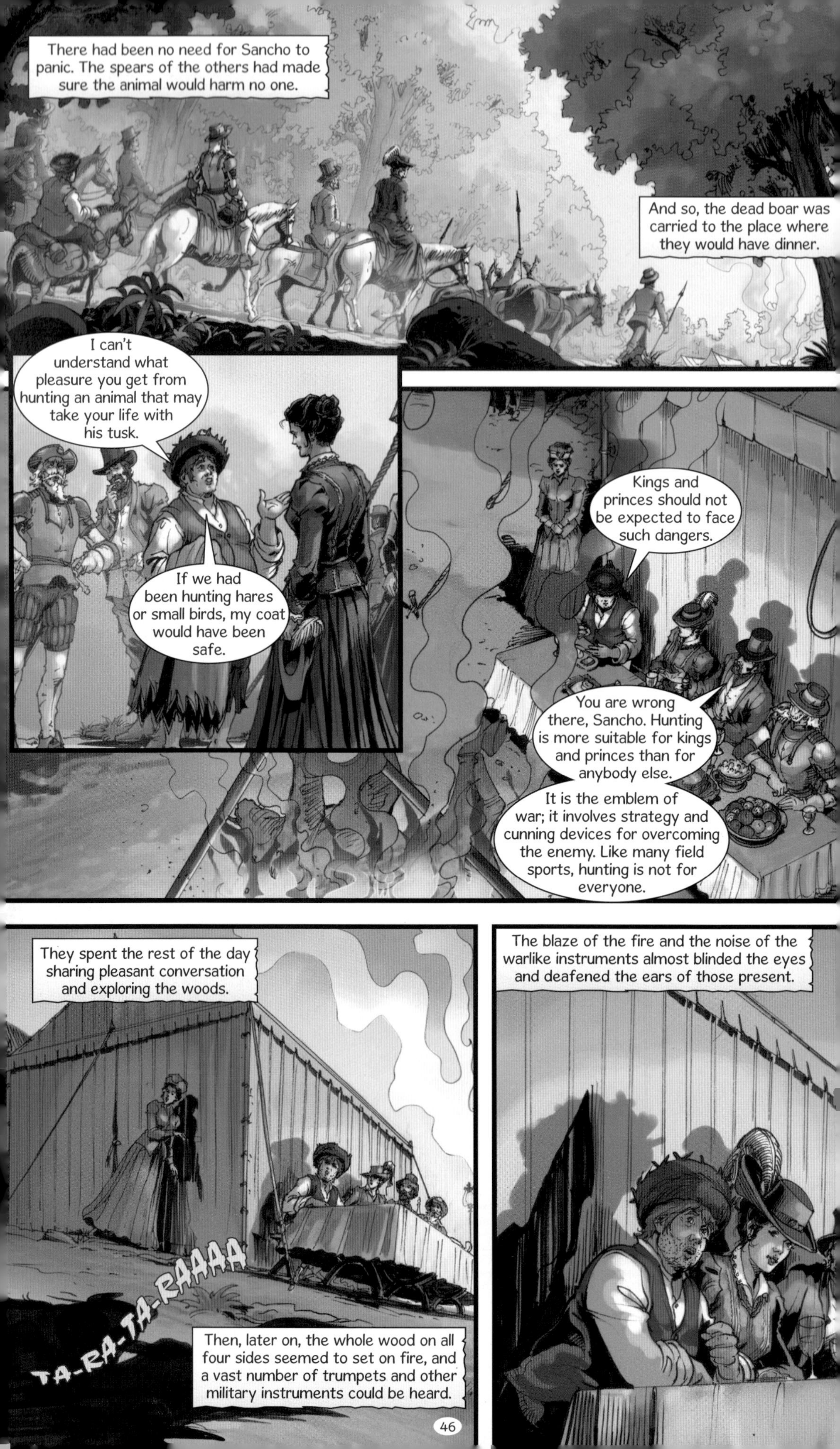

There had been no need for Sancho to panic. The spears of the others had made sure the animal would harm no one.
And so, the dead boar was carried to the place where they would have dinner.
I can't understand what pleasure you get from hunting an animal that may take your life with his tusk.
If we had been hunting hares or small birds, my coat would have been safe.
Kings and princes should not be expected to face such dangers.
You are wrong there, Sancho. Hunting is more suitable for kings and princes than for anybody else.
It is the emblem of war; it involves strategy and cunning devices for overcoming the enemy. Like many field sports, hunting is not for everyone.
They spent the rest of the day sharing pleasant conversation and exploring the woods.
TA-RA-TA-RAAAA
Then, later on, the whole wood on all four sides seemed to set on fire, and a vast number of trumpets and other military instruments could be heard.
The blaze of the fire and the noise of the warlike instruments almost blinded the eyes and deafened the ears of those present.

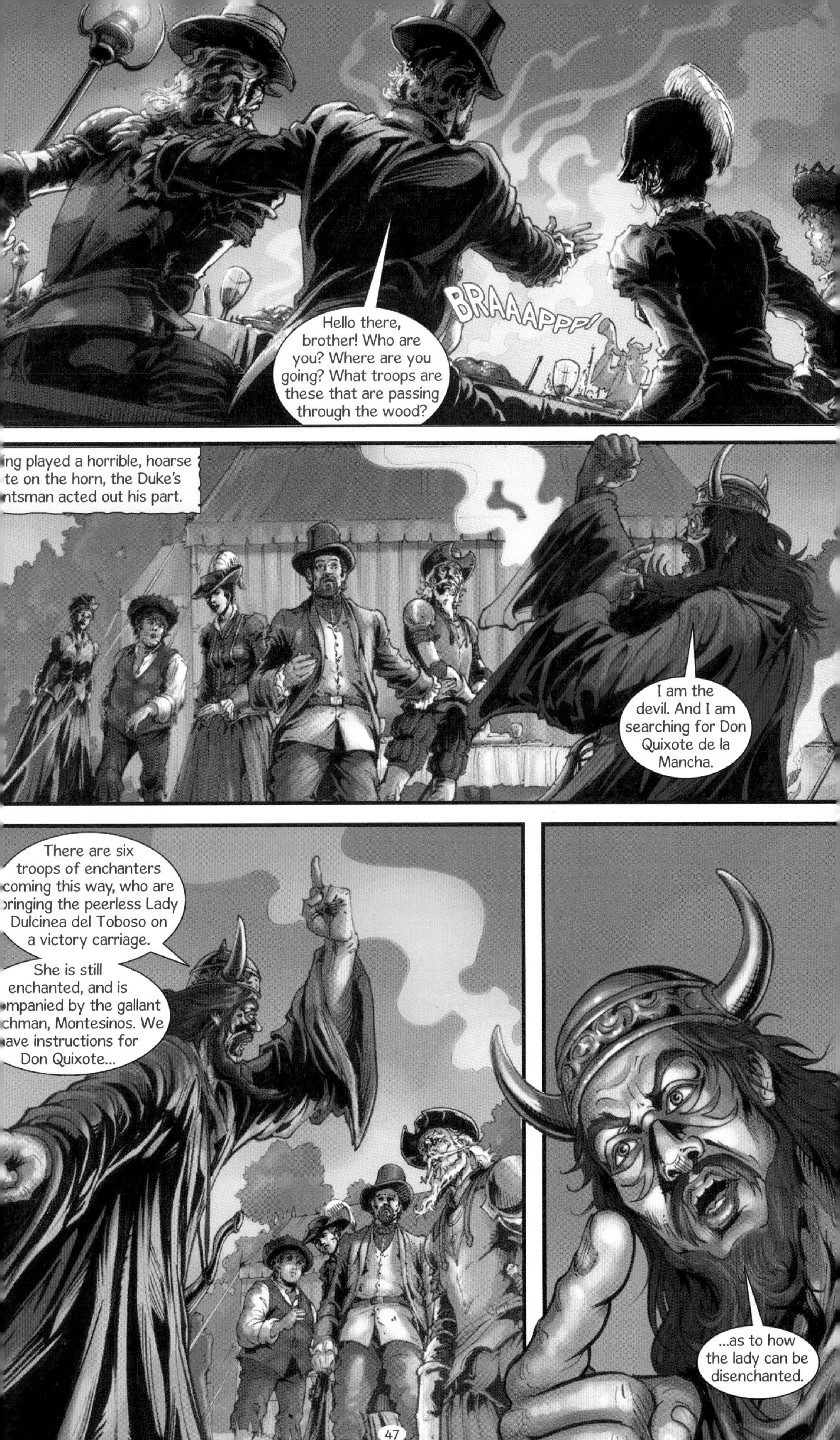
BRAAAPPP!
Hello there, brother! Who are you? Where are you going? What troops are these that are passing through the wood?
ing played a horrible, hoarse te on the horn, the Duke's ntsman acted out his part.
I am the devil. And I am searching for Don Quixote de la Mancha.
There are six troops of enchanters coming this way, who are bringing the peerless Lady Dulcinea del Toboso on a victory carriage.
She is still enchanted, and is mpanied by the gallant chman, Montesinos. We ave instructions for Don Quixote...
...as to how the lady can be disenchanted.

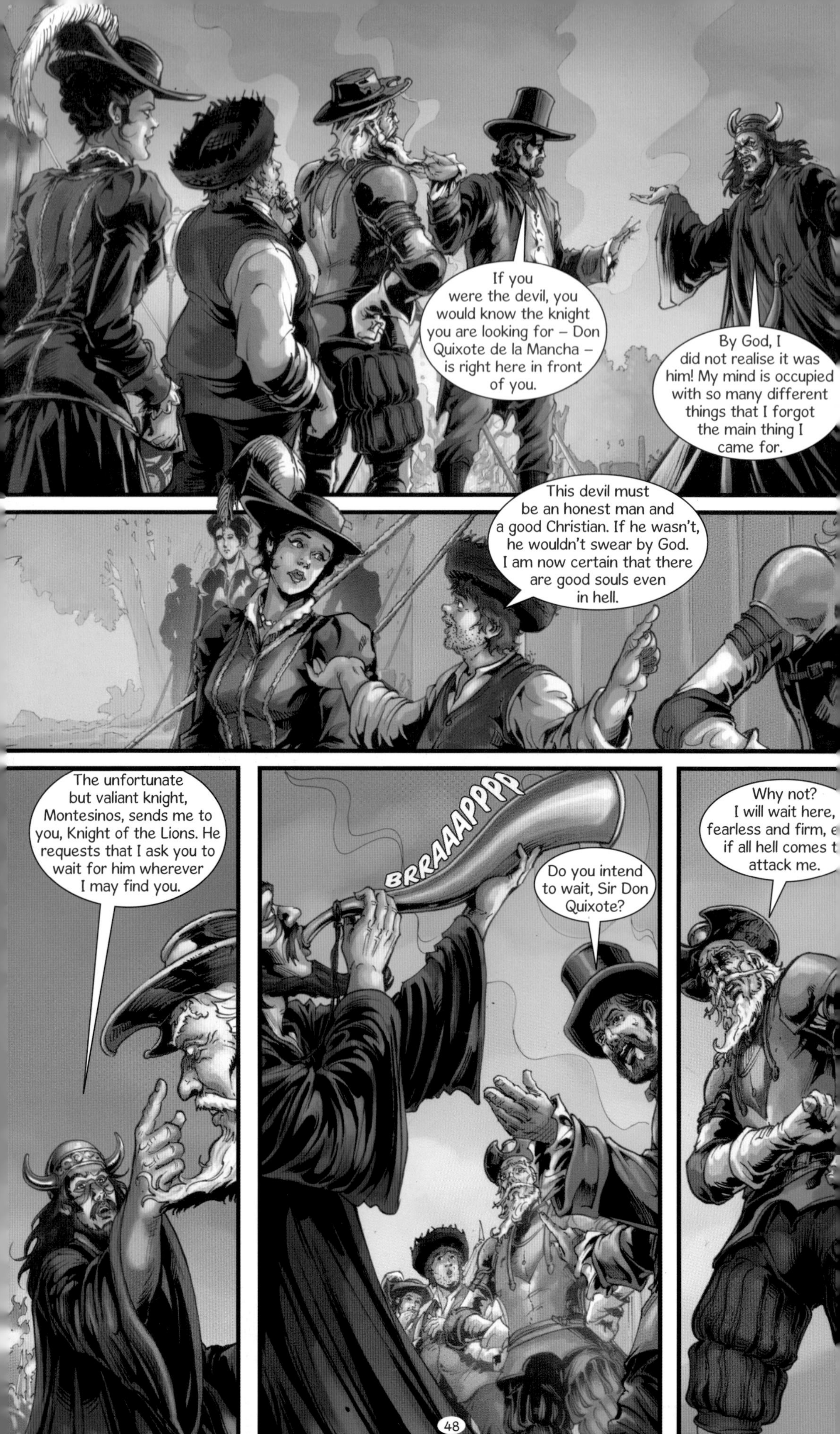
If you were the devil, you would know the knight you are looking for – Don Quixote de la Mancha – is right here in front of you.
By God, I did not realise it was him! My mind is occupied with so many different things that I forgot the main thing I came for.
This devil must be an honest man and a good Christian. If he wasn't, he wouldn't swear by God. I am now certain that there are good souls even in hell.
The unfortunate but valiant knight, Montesinos, sends me to you, Knight of the Lions. He requests that I ask you to wait for him wherever I may find you.
BRRAAAPPPP
Do you intend to wait, Sir Don Quixote?
Why not? I will wait here, fearless and firm, e
if all hell comes t
attack me.

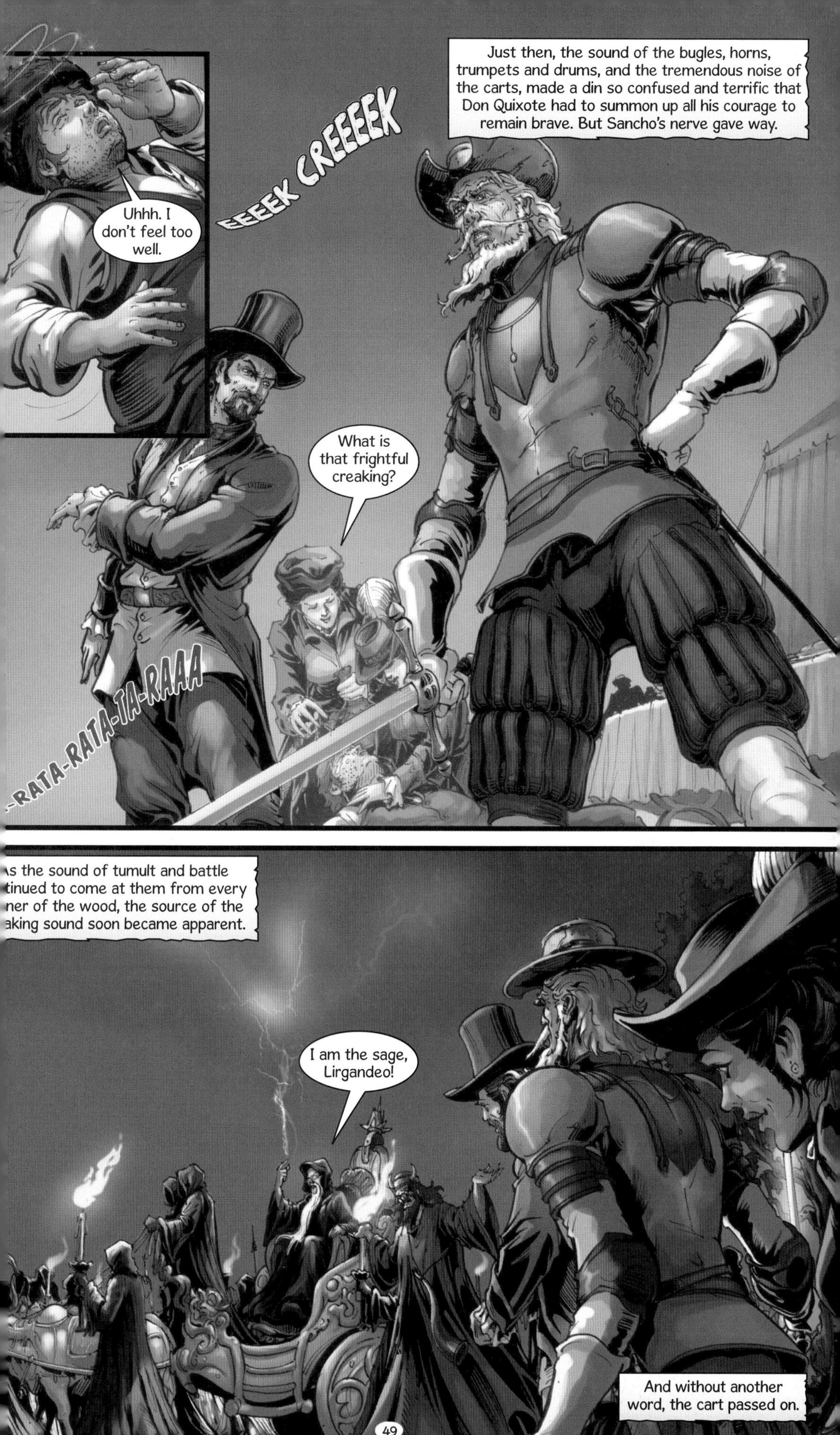

Just then, the sound of the bugles, horns, trumpets and drums, and the tremendous noise of the carts, made a din so confused and terrific that Don Quixote had to summon up all his courage to remain brave. But Sancho's nerve gave way.
EEEEK CREEEEK
Uhhh. I don't feel too well.
What is that frightful creaking?
-RATA-RATA-TA-RAAA
ʌs the sound of tumult and battle tinued to come at them from every ner of the wood, the source of the aking sound soon became apparent.
I am the sage, Lirgandeo!
And without another word, the cart passed on.

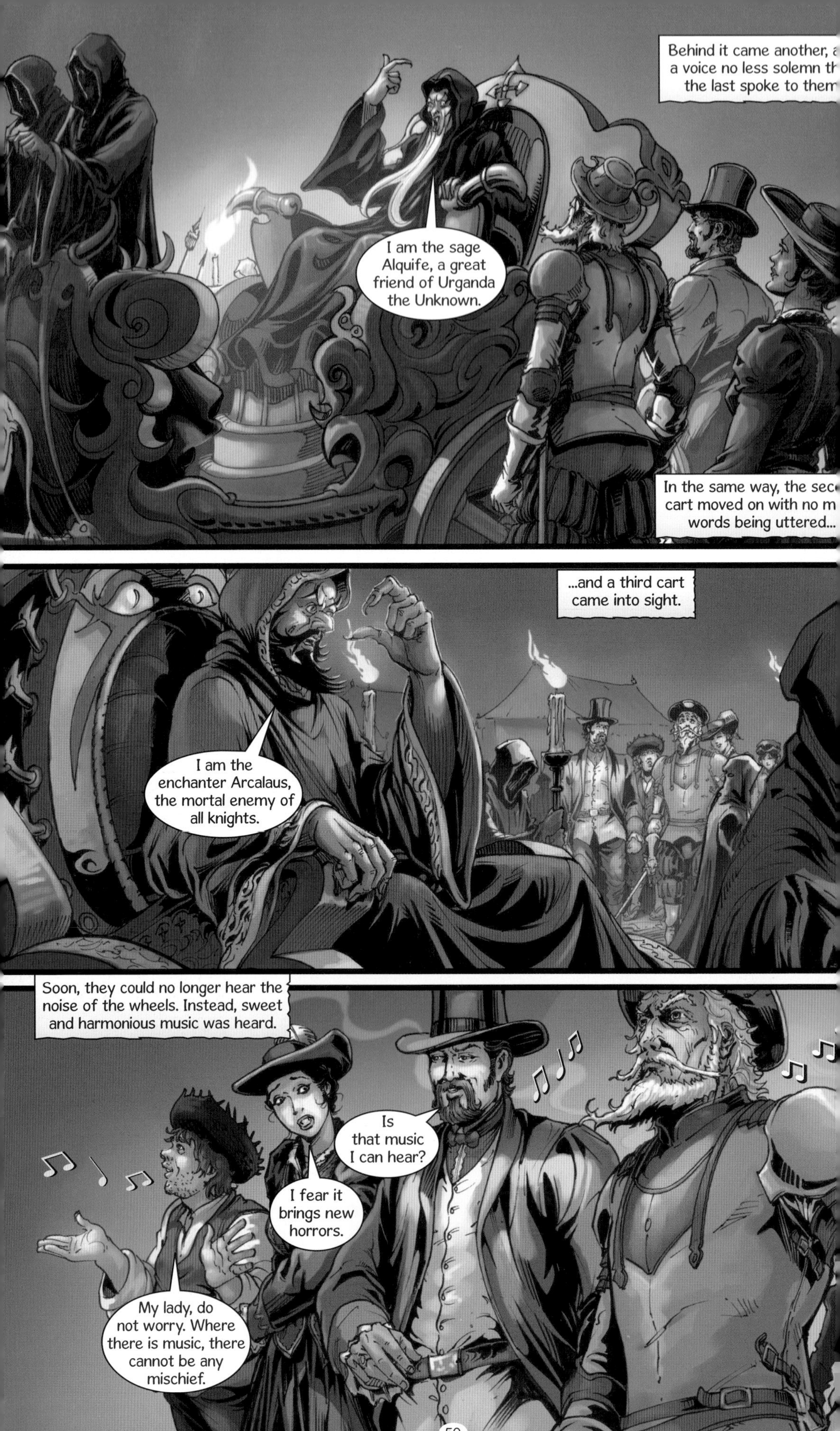

Behind it came another,
a voice no less solemn
the last spoke to
I am the sage Alquife, a great friend of Urganda the Unknown.
In the same way, the se
cart moved on with no
words being uttered...
...and a third cart came into sight.
I am the enchanter Arcalaus, the mortal enemy of all knights.
Soon, they could no longer hear the noise of the wheels. Instead, sweet and harmonious music was heard.
Is that music I can hear?
I fear it brings new horrors.
My lady, do not worry. Where there is music, there cannot be any mischief.

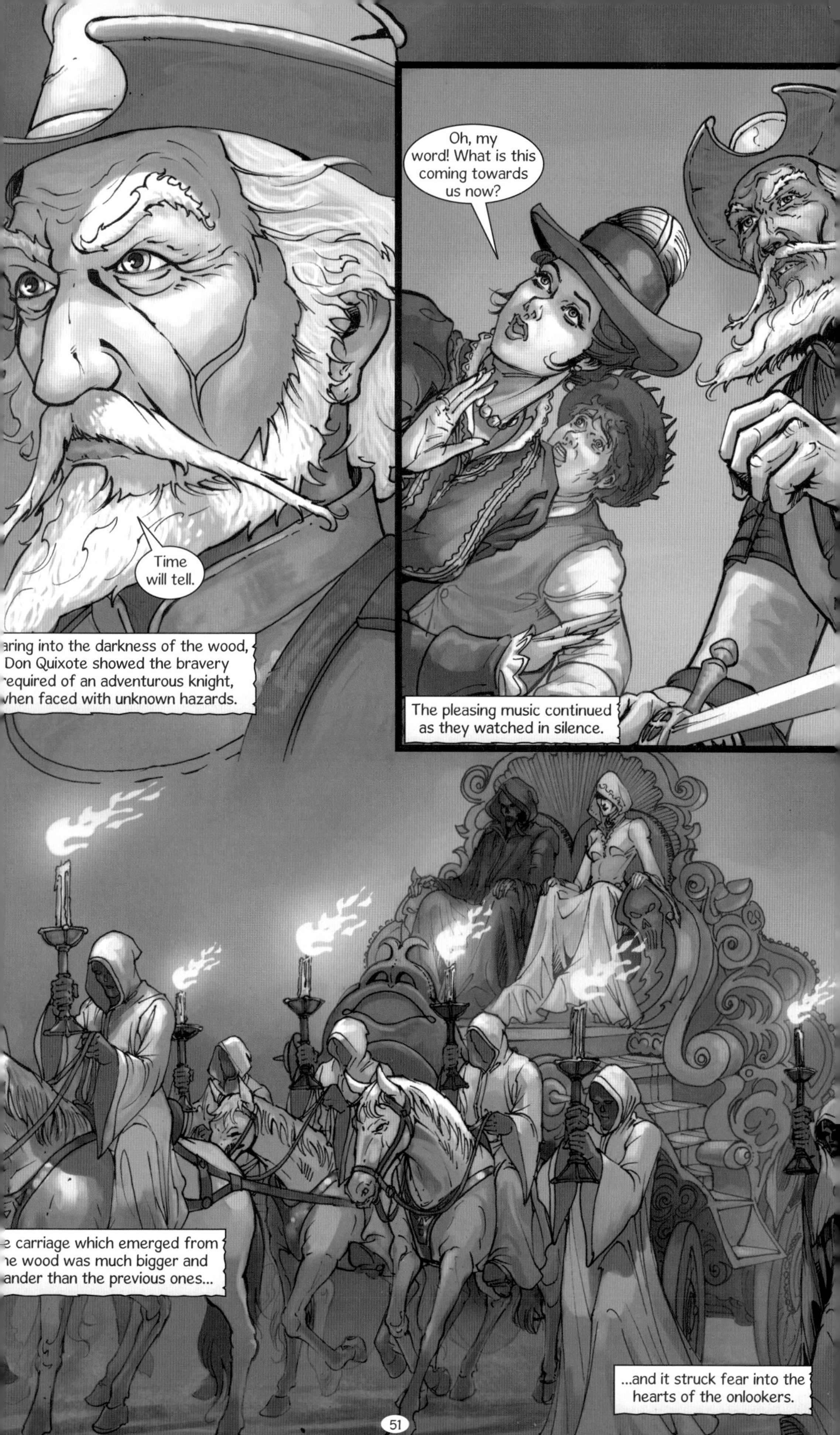
Time will tell.
aring into the darkness of the wood, Don Quixote showed the bravery required of an adventurous knight, when faced with unknown hazards.
Oh, my word! What is this coming towards us now?
The pleasing music continued as they watched in silence.
e carriage which emerged from he wood was much bigger and ander than the previous ones...
...and it struck fear into the hearts of the onlookers.

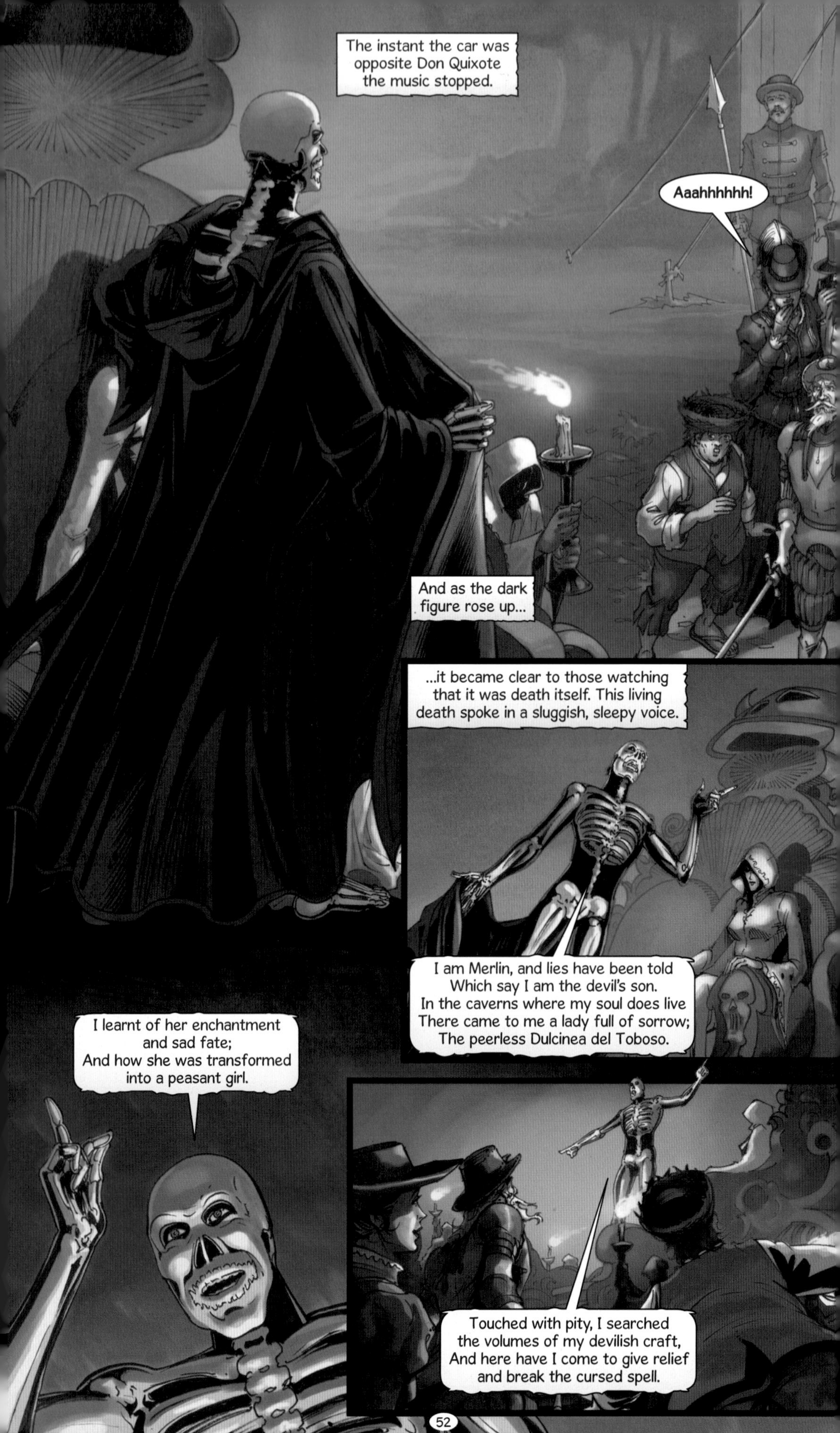

The instant the car was opposite Don Quixote the music stopped.
Aaahhhhhh!
And as the dark figure rose up...
...it became clear to those watching that it was death itself. This living death spoke in a sluggish, sleepy voice.
I am Merlin, and lies have been told Which say I am the devil's son. In the caverns where my soul does live There came to me a lady full of sorrow; The peerless Dulcinea del Toboso.
I learnt of her enchantment and sad fate; And how she was transformed into a peasant girl.
Touched with pity, I searched the volumes of my devilish craft, And here have I come to give relief and break the cursed spell.

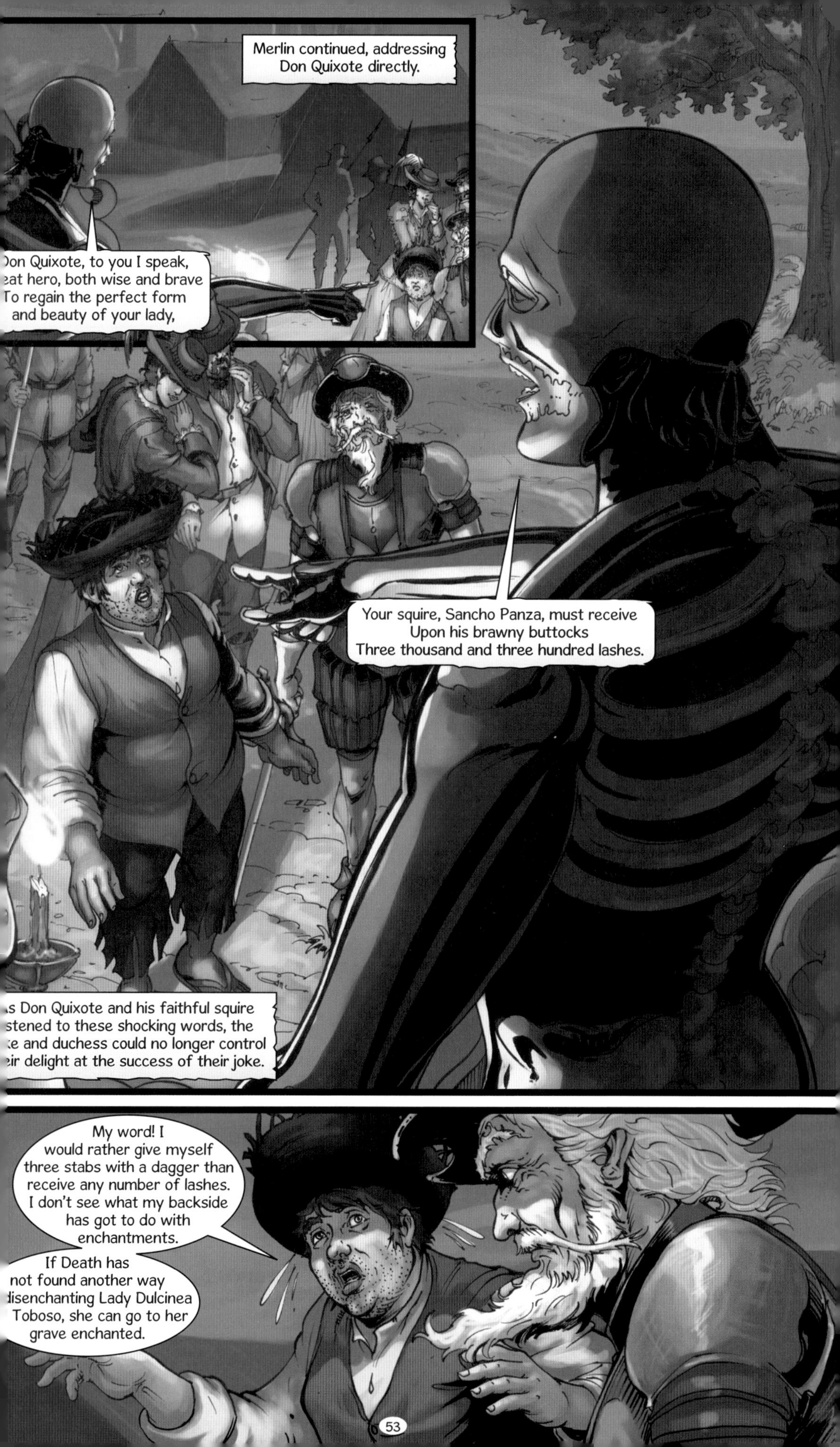
Merlin continued, addressing Don Quixote directly.
Don Quixote, to you I speak, eat hero, both wise and brave To regain the perfect form and beauty of your lady,
Your squire, Sancho Panza, must receive Upon his brawny buttocks Three thousand and three hundred lashes.
s Don Quixote and his faithful squire stened to these shocking words, the ke and duchess could no longer control eir delight at the success of their joke.
My word! I would rather give myself three stabs with a dagger than receive any number of lashes. I don't see what my backside has got to do with enchantments.
If Death has not found another way isenchanting Lady Dulcinea Toboso, she can go to her grave enchanted.

How dare you! I will stuff you with garlic, you clown, and tie you to a tree as naked as the day you were born. Then I'll give you six thousand six hundred lashes, never mind three thousand three hundred!

Don't say a word or I'll tear your soul out.

That would be no good. The lashes Sancho has to receive must be given of his own free will and not by force, and at whatever time he pleases, as there is no fixed limit.

Not a hand shall touch me! Did I give birth to the lady Dulcinea del Toboso, so that my backside now has to pay for her sins?

No sooner had Sancho Panza ceased to speak than the nymph, who had been silent until then, stood forward.

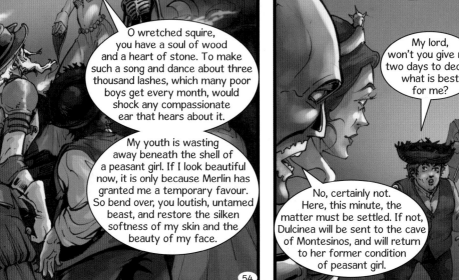

O wretched squire, you have a soul of wood and a heart of stone. To make such a song and dance about three thousand lashes, which many poor boys get every month, would shock any compassionate ear that hears about it.

My youth is wasting away beneath the shell of a peasant girl. If I look beautiful now, it is only because Merlin has granted me a temporary favour. So bend over, you loutish, untamed beast, and restore the silken softness of my skin and the beauty of my face.

Dulcinea speaks truth

My lord, won't you give me two days to decide what is best for me?

No, certainly not. Here, this minute, the matter must be settled. If not, Dulcinea will be sent to the cave of Montesinos, and will return to her former condition of peasant girl.

54

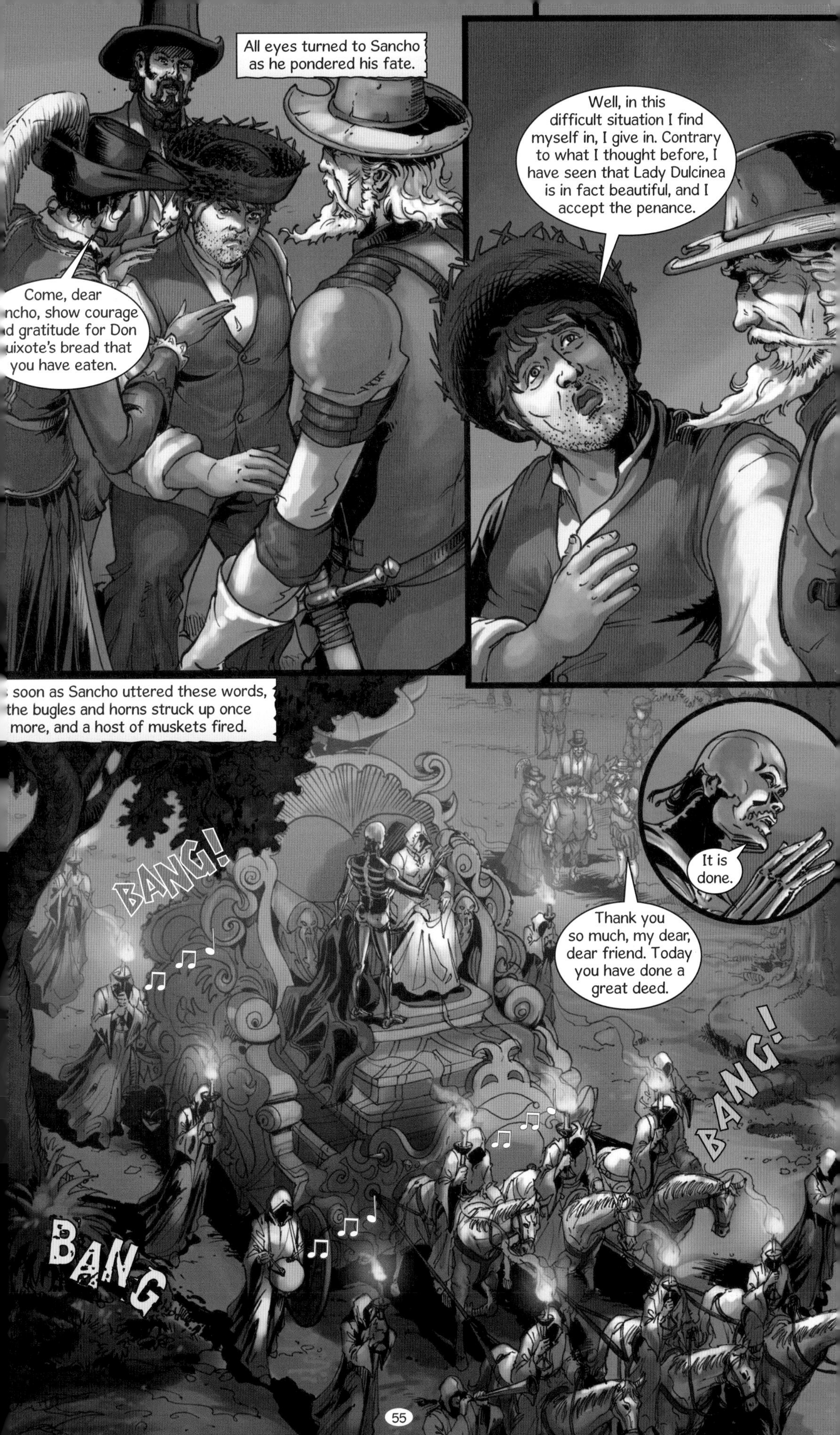
All eyes turned to Sancho as he pondered his fate.
Come, dear ncho, show courage d gratitude for Don uixote's bread that you have eaten.
Well, in this difficult situation I find myself in, I give in. Contrary to what I thought before, I have seen that Lady Dulcinea is in fact beautiful, and I accept the penance.
soon as Sancho uttered these words, the bugles and horns struck up once more, and a host of muskets fired.
It is done.
Thank you so much, my dear, dear friend. Today you have done a great deed.
BANG!
BANG!
BANG

The duke and duchess were pleased that their plan had been carried out so cleverly and successfully. And as they returned to the castle, they decided to follow up their joke to continue the amusement.

The duke's steward, a comical fellow, had played the part of Merlin and arranged the whole pageant. He had also written the words and got a page to play Lady Dulcinea.

And as the hunting party made their way back to the castle the steward prepared another trick – the most amusing and strangest imaginable.

The following day, Sancho and the duchess made their way to yet another sumptuous feast.

Tell me, dear Sancho, have you begun your penance yet?

Oh yes, ma'am, I have. I gave myself five lashes last night.

What did you give them with?

With my hand.

Your hand! That is more like giving yourself slaps than lashes Sancho. Father Merlin will not be satisfied with such a gentle approach. You should lash yourself with something that will hurt.

owing dinner, Sancho's rich conversation entertained all those present for a while. But then the sad and scordant sound of a fife and drum became audible.

BOOM BOOM

The conversation stopped, and all es turned towards the figure, who approached them with dignity, his eps matching the beat of the drum.

Most high and mighty senor, my name is Trifaldin of the White Beard. I m squire to Countess Trifaldi, also known as the Distressed Duenna. I bring a message on her behalf, requesting permission for her to come and tell Your Highness about her troubles.

But first, she wants to know if the valiant knight, Don Quixote de la Mancha, is in this castle. She has walked all the way from the kingdom of Kandy, without food, in search of him.

We have heard of this lady's misfortunes, and how the enchanters have caused her to be called the Distressed Duenna. Don Quixote is here, and he will assist and protect her. Bring her in.

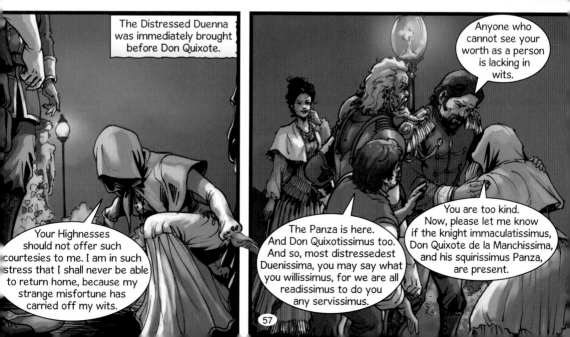

The Distressed Duenna was immediately brought before Don Quixote.

Your Highnesses should not offer such courtesies to me. I am in such stress that I shall never be able to return home, because my strange misfortune has carried off my wits.

Anyone who cannot see your worth as a person is lacking in wits.

The Panza is here. And Don Quixotissimus too. And so, most distressedest Duenissima, you may say what you willissimus, for we are all readissimus to do you any servissimus.

You are too kind. Now, please let me know if the knight immaculatissimus, Don Quixote de la Manchissima, and his squirissimus Panza, are present.

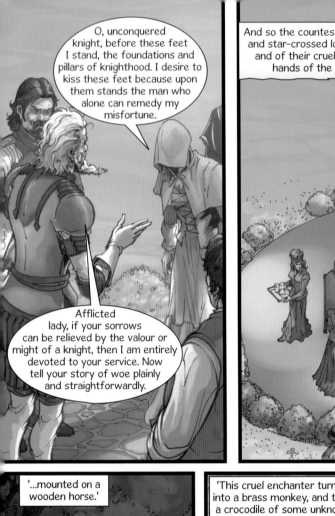

O, unconquered knight, before these feet I stand, the foundations and pillars of knighthood. I desire to kiss these feet because upon them stands the man who alone can remedy my misfortune.

Afflicted lady, if your sorrows can be relieved by the valour or might of a knight, then I am entirely devoted to your service. Now tell your story of woe plainly and straightforwardly.

And so the countess told a tale of deceptive and star-crossed lovers, a widowed queen, and of their cruel and tragic fate at the hands of the giant, Malambruno.

After the queen died, we buried her. We'd hardly covered her with earth and said our last farewells, when the giant Malambruno appeared...

'...mounted on a wooden horse.'

'He had come to punish the young lovers; the boy for his audacity and the girl for her frivolity.'

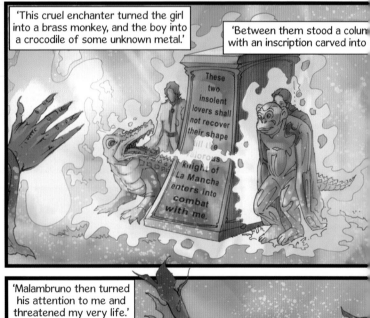

'This cruel enchanter turned the girl into a brass monkey, and the boy into a crocodile of some unknown metal.'

'Between them stood a colum with an inscription carved into

These two insolent lovers shall not recover their shape till the glorious knight of La Mancha enters into combat with me.

'Malambruno then turned his attention to me and threatened my very life.'

Pl-please don't kill me.

'He spared me, but ordered all the duennas of the palace, all of them present here today, to be brought before him.'

'As soon as he stopp speaking, we felt o faces start to chang

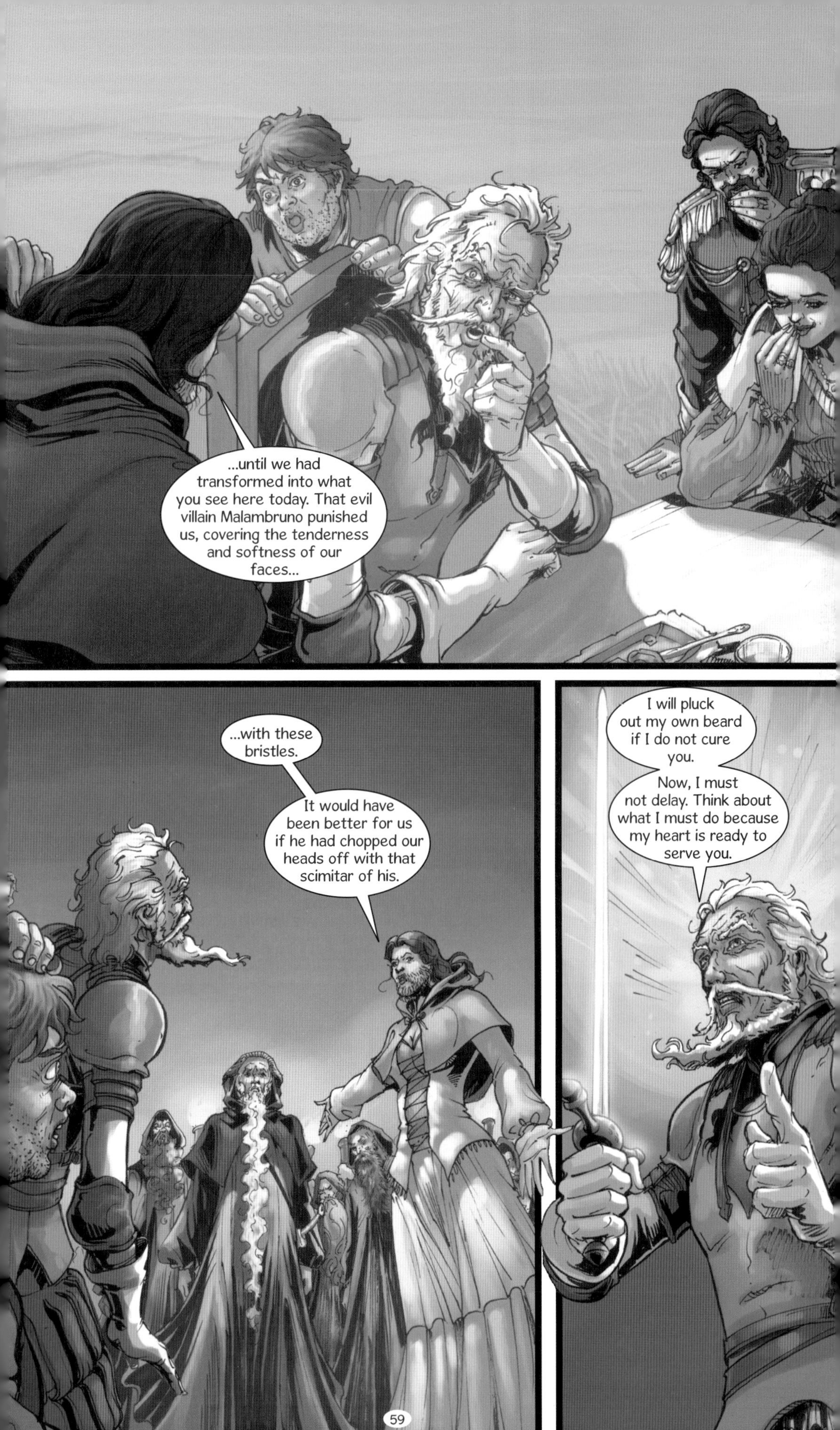
...until we had transformed into what you see here today. That evil villain Malambruno punished us, covering the tenderness and softness of our faces...
...with these bristles.
It would have been better for us if he had chopped our heads off with that scimitar of his.
I will pluck out my own beard if I do not cure you.
Now, I must not delay. Think about what I must do because my heart is ready to serve you.

It is too far to travel to my kingdom by land, so you must go through the air.

Malambruno told me that, when I found the knight to end our enchantment, he would send a famous horse – the horse which the giant himself uses.

His name is Clavileno the Swift, is made of wood, has a peg in his head to guide him, and travels through the air most rapidly.

And here he is.

Now let the knight, who has courage, mount machine.

That is not me, for I have no courage, nor am I a knight.

And let hi take his sq behind him, has one

Without hesitation, Don Quixote stepped forwards to mount Clavileno.

Turn this peg, and the horse will take you through the air to where Malambruno is waiting. And, so that you don't feel giddy during the journey, your eyes must be covered.

Don Quixote, finding himself settled to his satisfaction, felt for the peg.

God guide you, valiant knight!

God be with you, brave squire!

Mind you don't fall off.

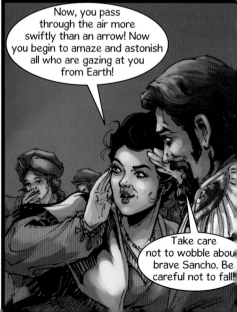

Now, you pass through the air more swiftly than an arrow! Now you begin to amaze and astonish all who are gazing at you from Earth!

Take care not to wobble abou brave Sancho. Be careful not to fall!

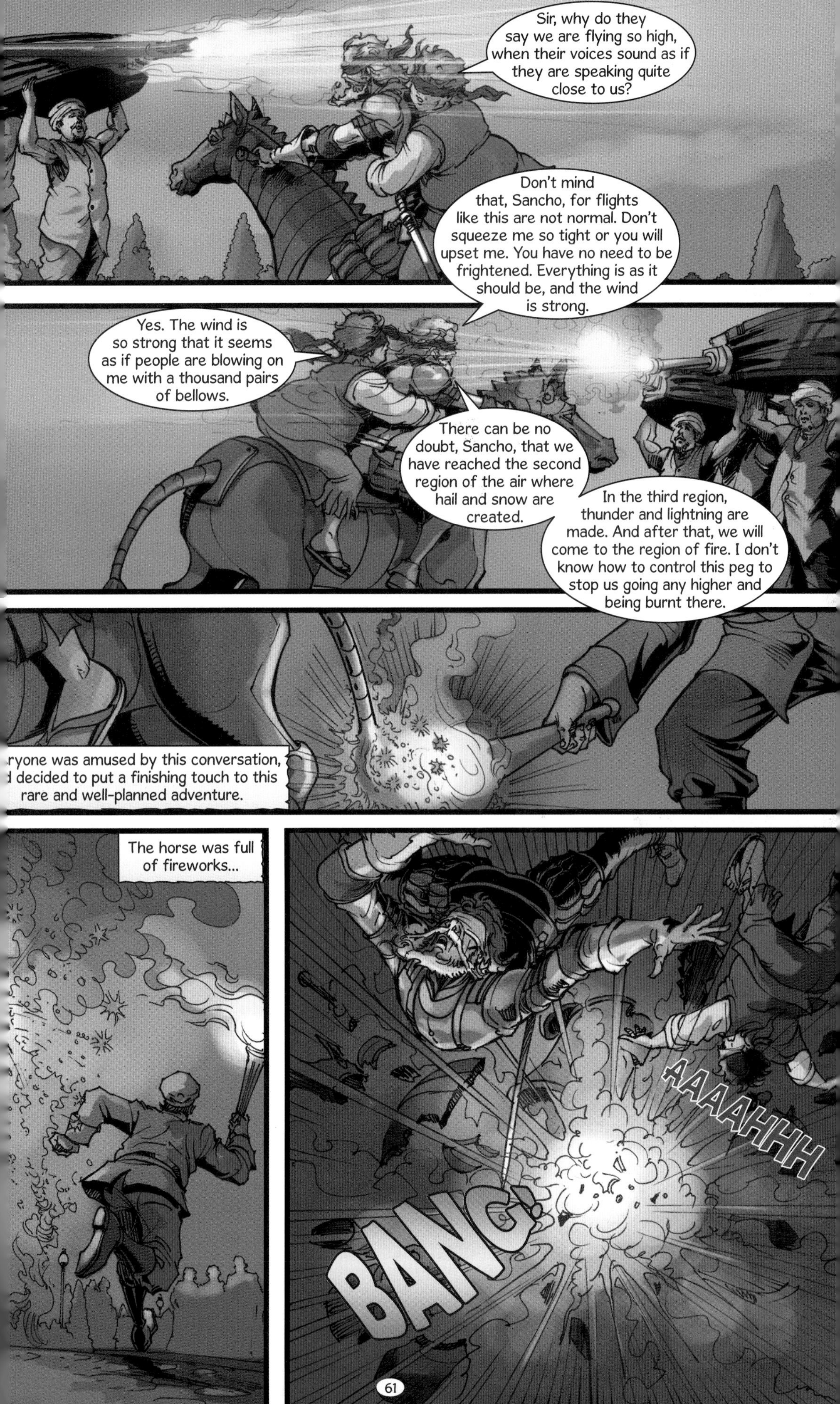

Sir, why do they say we are flying so high, when their voices sound as if they are speaking quite close to us?
Don't mind that, Sancho, for flights like this are not normal. Don't squeeze me so tight or you will upset me. You have no need to be frightened. Everything is as it should be, and the wind is strong.
Yes. The wind is so strong that it seems as if people are blowing on me with a thousand pairs of bellows.
There can be no doubt, Sancho, that we have reached the second region of the air where hail and snow are created.
In the third region, thunder and lightning are made. And after that, we will come to the region of fire. I don't know how to control this peg to stop us going any higher and being burnt there.
ryone was amused by this conversation, d decided to put a finishing touch to this rare and well-planned adventure.
The horse was full of fireworks...
AAAAHHH
BANG!

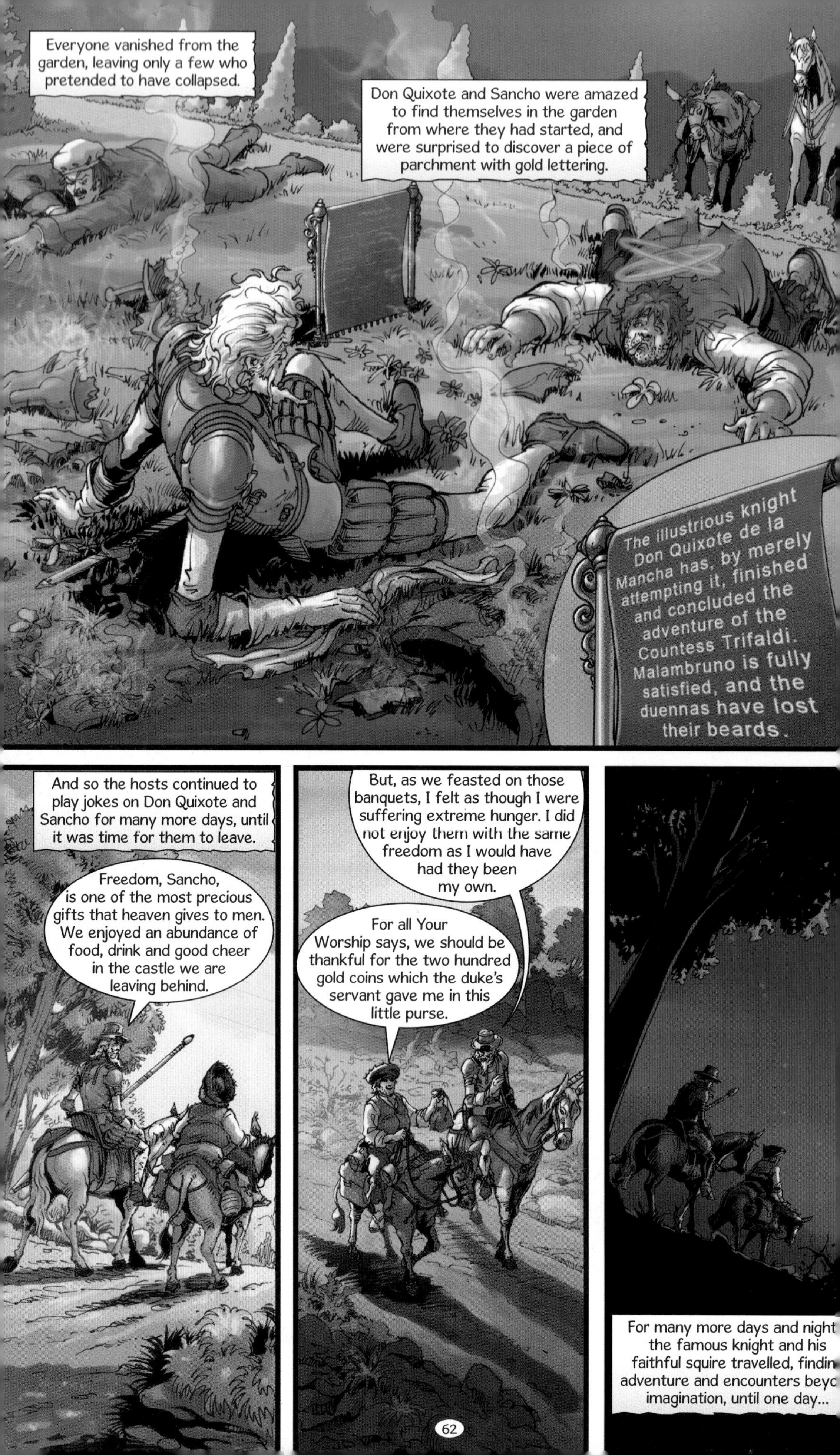
Everyone vanished from the garden, leaving only a few who pretended to have collapsed.
Don Quixote and Sancho were amazed to find themselves in the garden from where they had started, and were surprised to discover a piece of parchment with gold lettering.
The illustrious knight Don Quixote de la Mancha has, by merely attempting it, finished and concluded the adventure of the Countess Trifaldi. Malambruno is fully satisfied, and the duennas have lost their beards.
And so the hosts continued to play jokes on Don Quixote and Sancho for many more days, until it was time for them to leave.
Freedom, Sancho, is one of the most precious gifts that heaven gives to men. We enjoyed an abundance of food, drink and good cheer in the castle we are leaving behind.
But, as we feasted on those banquets, I felt as though I were suffering extreme hunger. I did not enjoy them with the same freedom as I would have had they been my own.
For all Your Worship says, we should be thankful for the two hundred gold coins which the duke's servant gave me in this little purse.
For many more days and night the famous knight and his faithful squire travelled, findin adventure and encounters beyo imagination, until one day...

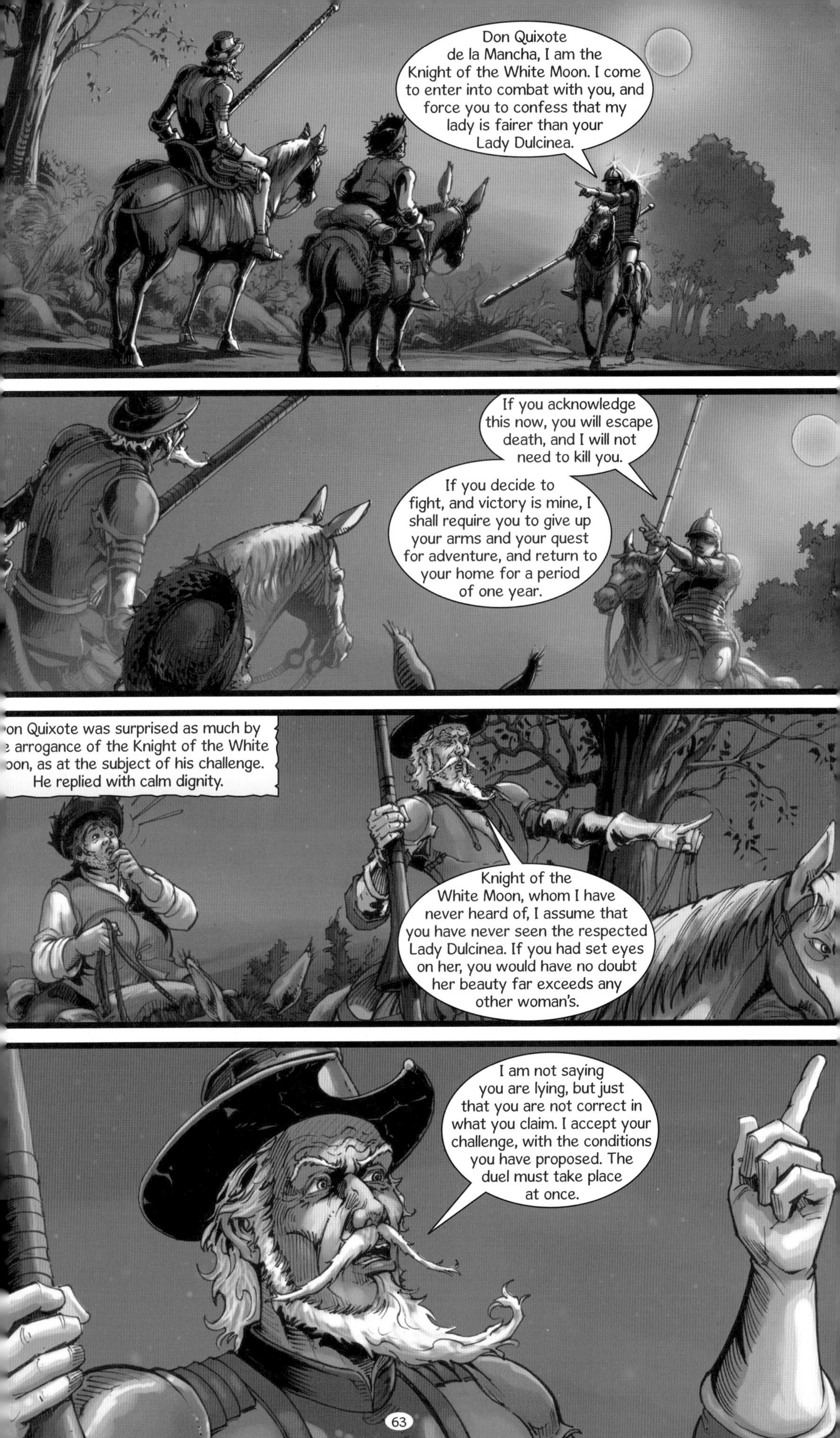
Don Quixote de la Mancha, I am the Knight of the White Moon. I come to enter into combat with you, and force you to confess that my lady is fairer than your Lady Dulcinea.
If you acknowledge this now, you will escape death, and I will not need to kill you.
If you decide to fight, and victory is mine, I shall require you to give up your arms and your quest for adventure, and return to your home for a period of one year.
on Quixote was surprised as much by e arrogance of the Knight of the White oon, as at the subject of his challenge. He replied with calm dignity.
Knight of the White Moon, whom I have never heard of, I assume that you have never seen the respected Lady Dulcinea. If you had set eyes on her, you would have no doubt her beauty far exceeds any other woman's.
I am not saying you are lying, but just that you are not correct in what you claim. I accept your challenge, with the conditions you have proposed. The duel must take place at once.

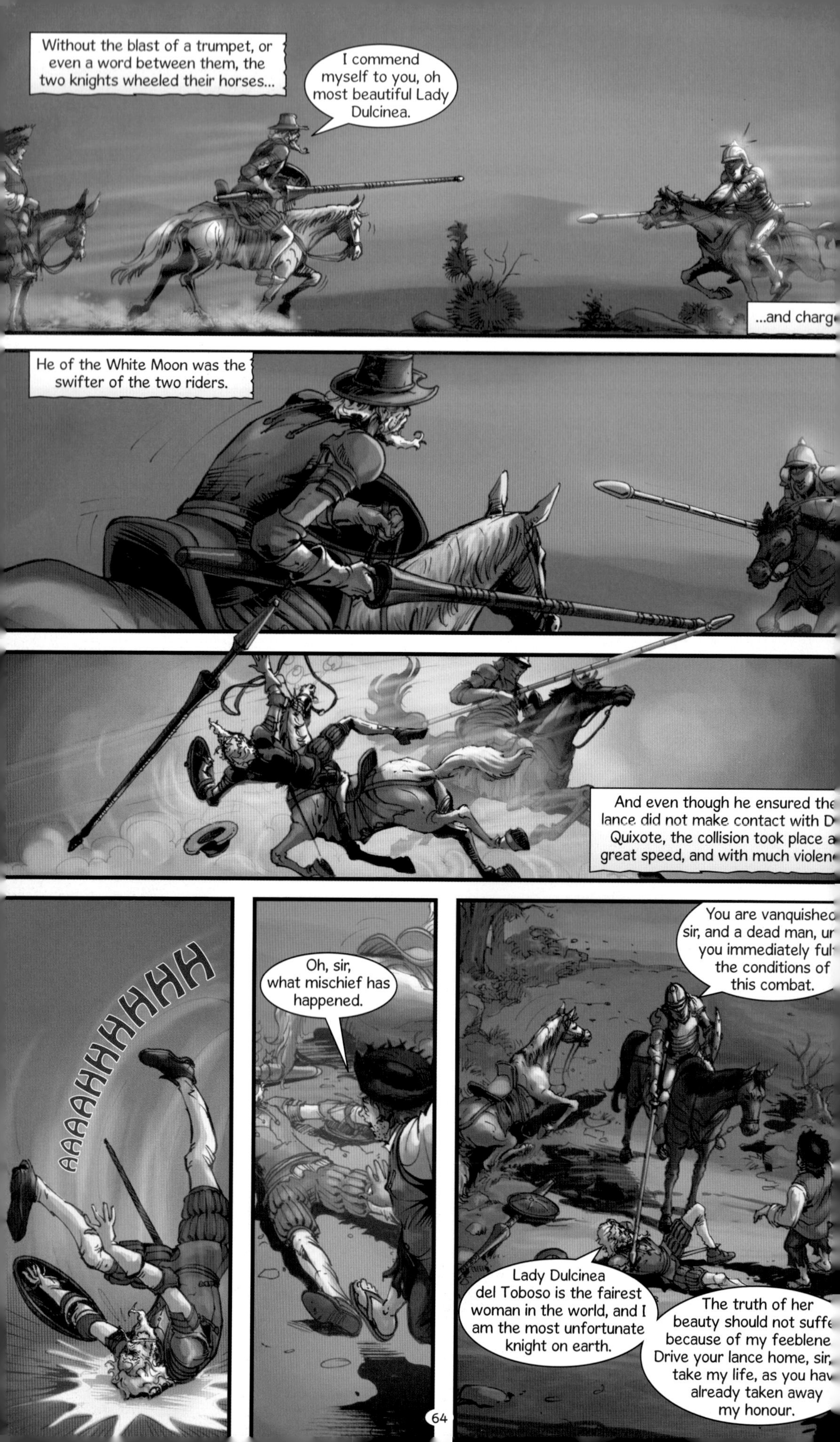

Without the blast of a trumpet, or even a word between them, the two knights wheeled their horses...
I commend myself to you, oh most beautiful Lady Dulcinea.
...and charg
He of the White Moon was the swifter of the two riders.
And even though he ensured the lance did not make contact with D Quixote, the collision took place a great speed, and with much violen
AAAAHHHHHH
Oh, sir, what mischief has happened.
You are vanquished sir, and a dead man, ur you immediately ful the conditions of this combat.
Lady Dulcinea del Toboso is the fairest woman in the world, and I am the most unfortunate knight on earth.
The truth of her beauty should not suffe because of my feeblene Drive your lance home, sir, take my life, as you hav already taken away my honour.

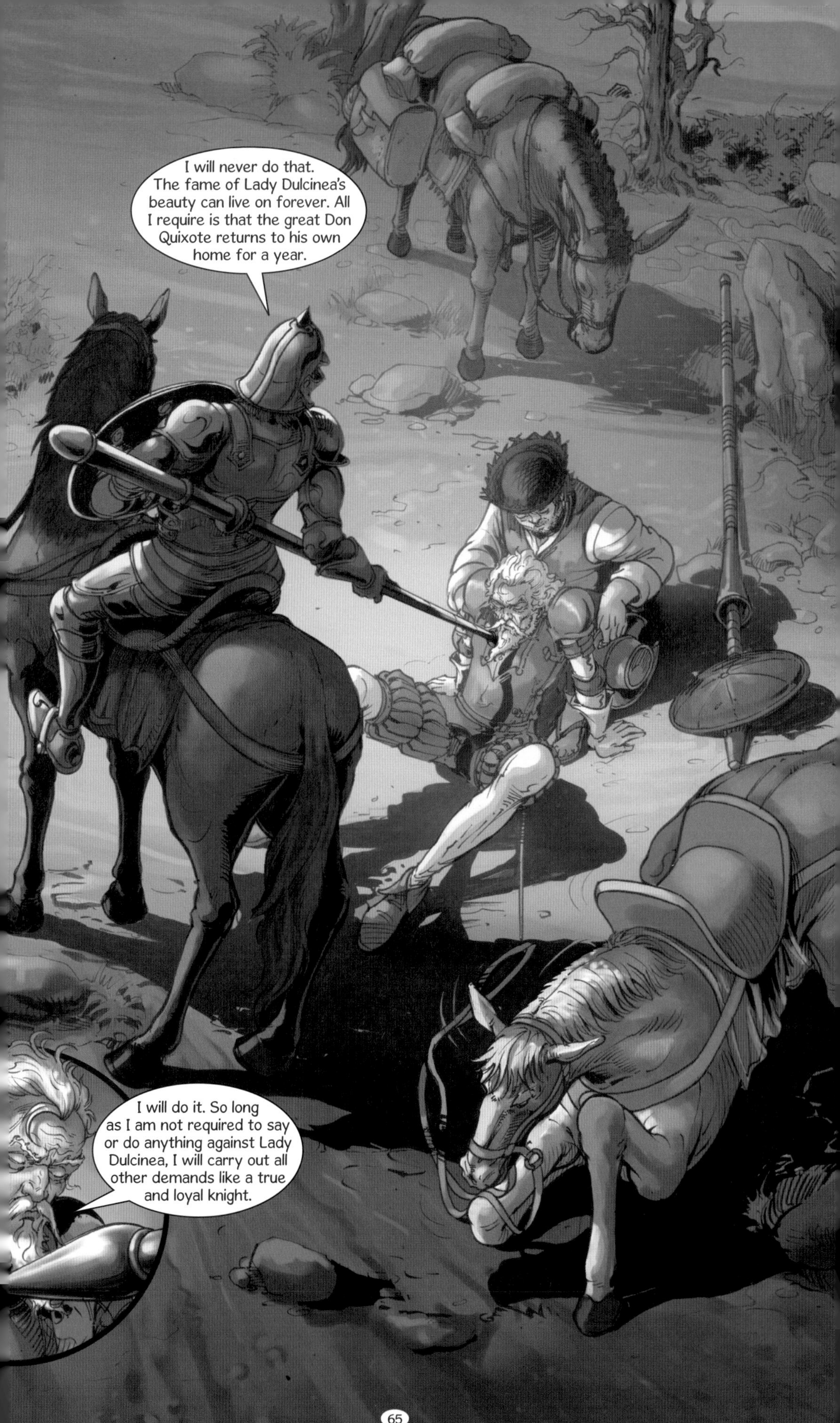
I will never do that. The fame of Lady Dulcinea's beauty can live on forever. All I require is that the great Don Quixote returns to his own home for a year.
I will do it. So long as I am not required to say or do anything against Lady Dulcinea, I will carry out all other demands like a true and loyal knight.

With this settled, the Knight of the White Moon had achieved his goal.

Feeling dejected, Sancho did not know what to say or do. It seemed like a dream to him, or a piece of enchantment. He was his master defeated, and not allowed to take up arms for a year.

He feared Rozinante was crippled for life, and his master's bones all broken. If the collision had only shaken him out of his madness, it would be a piece of luck.

Unknown to Don Quixote and Sancho, the Knight of the White Moon was none other than Samson Carrasco. To cure Don Quixote's madness, and to ensure he returned home peacefully, the bachelor had concocted this

For six days, Don Quixote stayed in bed – dejected, out of sorts, and brooding over his defeat.

Hold up your head, sir. Be cheerful, and give thanks to heaven that you did not come off with a broken rib.

Let us go home, and stop searching for adventures in strange lands. In truth, I am the greater loser, even though it is Your Worship who has been injured.

I do not want to be a governor anymore, but I hope to be a count one day. That will never happen if Your Worship gives up his chivalrous knighthood.

Peace, Sancho. My retirement is not to exceed a year. I will soon return to my honoured calling, and I will certainly win a kingdom and give you a county.

May God hear it and sin be deaf. Some hope is better than nothing.

And so, Don Quixote and Sancho left for home.

Here it was that my misfortune, not my cowardice, robbed me of all the glory I had won. Here fortune made me the victim of her whims. Here the lustre of my achievements was dimmed. Here my happiness fell, never to rise again.

Sir, brave hearts must be patient in hard times, just as they should be glad in good times.

They came to their hometown, and saw the curate and the bachelor Samson Carrasco approaching.

My dear Don Quixote, it is so good to see you again.

It is a pleasure to have you both back home.

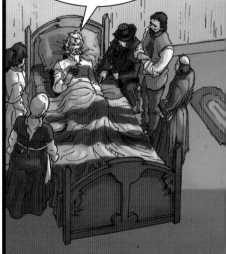

Don Quixote's niece and housekeeper were so pleased to see him, and even more pleased that he wanted to stay at home.

...and so, following so many victories, I finally tasted defeat. And that is why, as per the laws of knighthood, I have returned home to follow the instructions of the knight who vanquished me.

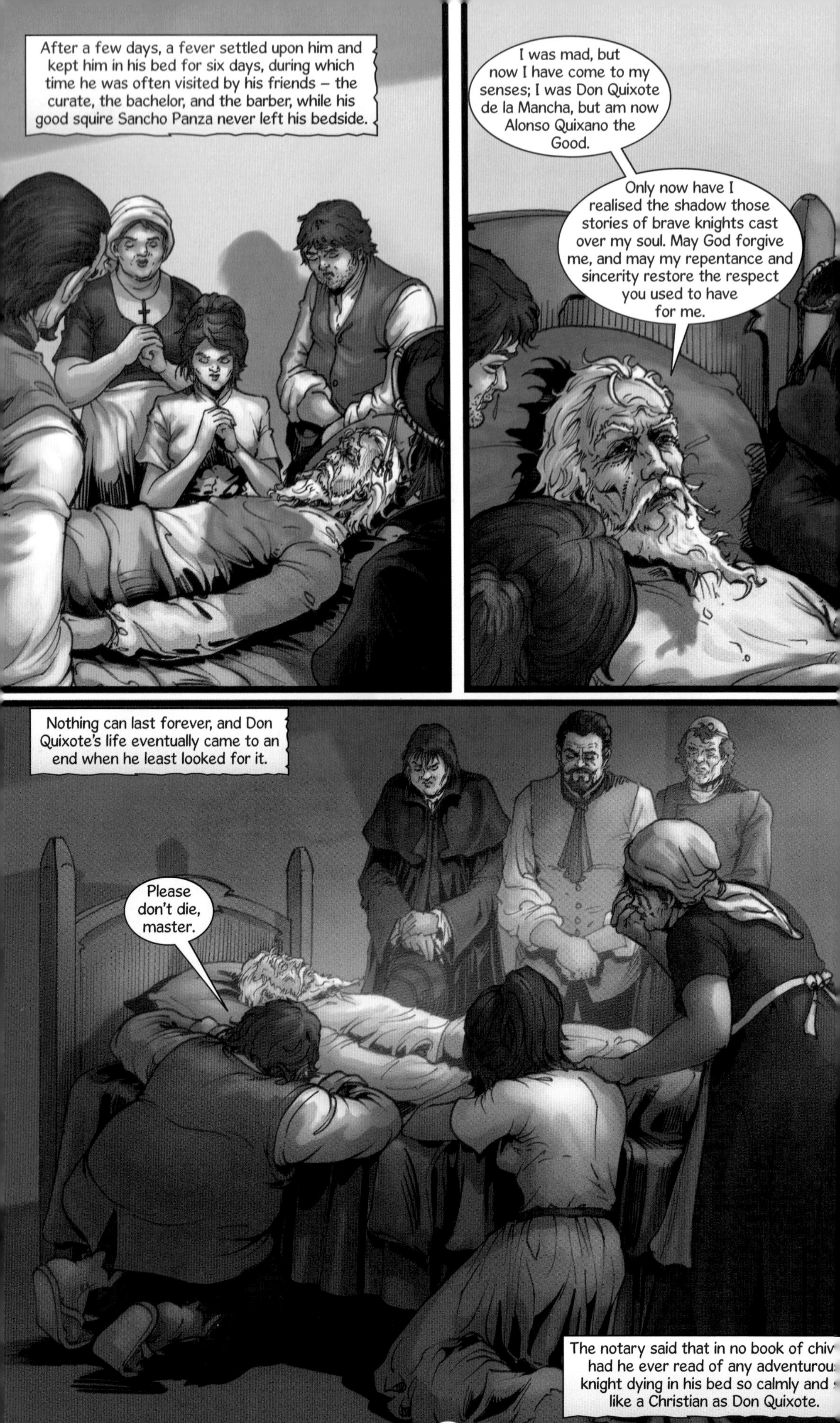
After a few days, a fever settled upon him and kept him in his bed for six days, during which time he was often visited by his friends – the curate, the bachelor, and the barber, while his good squire Sancho Panza never left his bedside.
I was mad, but now I have come to my senses; I was Don Quixote de la Mancha, but am now Alonso Quixano the Good.
Only now have I realised the shadow those stories of brave knights cast over my soul. May God forgive me, and may my repentance and sincerity restore the respect you used to have for me.
Nothing can last forever, and Don Quixote's life eventually came to an end when he least looked for it.
Please don't die, master.
The notary said that in no book of chiv
had he ever read of any adventurou
knight dying in his bed so calmly and
like a Christian as Don Quixote.

Miguel de Cervantes
DON QUIXOTE
PART I
ED BY LLOYD S WAGNER
ILLUSTRATED BY RICHARD KOHLRUS

Miguel de Cervantes

DON QUIXOTE

PART I

Adapted by Lloyd S Wagner

Illustrated by Richard Kohlrus

A delightful tale filled with humour, adventures... and misadventures!

Don Quixote – this name is universally known for the idealistic, possibly insane, wannabe knight as much as a masterpiece of literature. *Don Quixote*, the book, is widely regarded as the first modern novel while Don Quixote, the character, is among the most recognisable and loveable ever created.

The author, Miguel de Cervantes, once said of Don Quixote that he was created so 'that children may handle him, youths may read him, men may understand him and old men may celebrate him.' Truly, the misadventures of Don Quixote and his faithful squire, Sancho Panza, are comic and entertaining to readers of all ages. At the same time, they speak deeply of man's place in the world, and of his aspirations.

This Campfire graphic novel adaptation is the ideal introduction to a story that readers will return to again and again throughout their lifetime – to read it, revel in it and love it.

MPFIRE™
ww.campfire.co.in

WHAT IS DELUSIONAL DISORDER?

Delusional disorder is a mental condition where someone has a very strong, fixed belief about something that is imaginary. The belief is so strong that logic and reason cannot have an effect on it.

DO YOU SEE WHAT I SEE?

Now, we're not saying that you are delusional, but we can certainly make you feel that way with some funny optical illusions! But, before that, let's find out what illusions are. The word 'illusion' is used to describe something that deceives by producing a false or misleading impression of reality. An example of an illusion is a mirage.

WHAT IS A MIRAGE?

If you are driving along a stretch of road on a hot, sunny day, it is quite likely that your eyes will see a puddle of water in the distance. However, when you get to the spot where you saw the water, you will realise that there is nothing there. This is an example of a mirage. A mirage is an optical phenomenon that creates the illusion of water. It is caused by the distortion of light rays as a result of alternate layers of hot and cool air.

OPTICAL ILLUSIONS

Optical illusions are visuals that cause a false or misleading impression. They are images that trick us into seeing things that aren't actually there. For example, if you stare at a moving fan, after a while it might start to look like it is rotating in the opposite direction! This is the kind of optical illusion you might see in daily life. And, sometimes, what you see might be different from what other people see! Don't believe us? Try the following:

CAN YOU TELL HOW MANY LEGS THIS ELEPHANT HAS? LOOK CAREFULLY! IT'S NOT AS EASY AS YOU THINK IT IS!

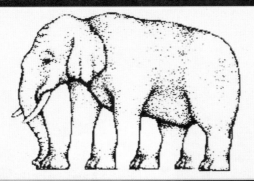

Ans: Just like every other elephant, this one has four legs! But you're bound to see more. It just depends on the way you look at it!

LOOK AT THE IMAGE BELOW. ARE THE LINES PARALLEL OR CROOKED?

Ans: They are parallel! If you don't believe us, take out your ruler and see for yourself!

TIME TO PLAY WITH WORDS! WHAT DO YOU SEE - GOOD OR EVIL?

Ans: Both 'GOOD' and 'EVIL' can be seen in this image. What you see depends on how you look at it.

Available now

Putting the fun back into reading!